CITYSPOTS
SEVILLE

Nick Inman

Thomas Cook

GW00546749

Written by Nick Inman
Original photography by Nick Inman
Front cover photography © Glen Allison/Alamy Images
Series design based on an original concept by Studio 183 Limited

Produced by Cambridge Publishing Management Limited
Project Editor: Rachel Wood
Layout: Trevor Double
Maps: PC Graphics
Transport maps: © Communicarta Limited

Published by Thomas Cook Publishing
A division of Thomas Cook Tour Operations Limited
Company Registration No. 1450464 England
PO Box 227, Unit 18, Coningsby Road
Peterborough PE3 8SB, United Kingdom
email: books@thomascook.com
www.thomascookpublishing.com
+ 44 (0) 1733 416477
ISBN-13: 978-1-84157-644-2
ISBN-10: 1-84157-644-1

First edition © 2006 Thomas Cook Publishing
Text © 2006 Thomas Cook Publishing
Maps © 2006 Thomas Cook Publishing
Series Editor: Kelly Anne Pipes
Project Editor: Ross Hilton
Production/DTP: Steven Collins

Printed and bound in Spain by GraphyCems

CONTENTS

SYMBOLS & ABBREVIATIONS

The following symbols are used throughout this book:

ⓐ address   ⓣ telephone   ⓕ fax   ⓔ email   ⓦ website address
ⓛ opening times   ⓝ public transport connections   ⓘ important

The following symbols are used on the maps:

🅹 information office		O	city
✈ airport		O	large town
➕ hospital		◦	small town
🛡 police station		═	motorway
🚌 bus station		—	main road
🚆 railway station		—	minor road
Ⓜ metro		—	railway
✝ cathedral			
❶ numbers denote featured cafés & restaurants			

Hotels and restaurants are graded by approximate price as follows:
£ budget   **££** mid-range   **£££** expensive

▶ *A shady corner at the Casa de Pilatos*

Introduction

If any city can encapsulate the colour, sensuality, carefreeness and vitality of southern Europe, it has to be Seville. It's a place that leaves few visitors cold. Rather most of them feel compelled towards glowing superlatives. Camilo José Cela, Spain's Nobel Prize-winning novelist, declared it a city capable of inspiring even the dullest of poets. The travel writer Nina Epton, meanwhile, observed that 'the most abstemious of visitors feels inebriated in Seville'.

Spain's fourth largest city and the capital of the region of Andalucia, it's the only city in the country to sit astride a major river, the great, green-flowing Guadalquivir river, 60 navigable kilometres (37 miles) inland from the Atlantic coast.

Seville's long and eventful history – particularly the days when gold flowed incessantly from Spain's New World colonies – has left it stuffed with innumerable monuments. Most conspicuous of them is the Giralda tower, which rises out of the cathedral as a Muslim minaret below and finishes as a Christian belfry.

Down at ground level, the biggest draws are the exquisite palace of the Reales Alcázares; the quaint Barrio de Santa Cruz, a perfect cluster of narrow shady streets through which the fragrance of orange blossom wafts in spring; the legendary Maestranza bullring; and, more ethereally, the music, passion and song of flamenco whose presence is felt all over the city. Such are the ingredients that gave birth to the fictional characters of Carmen and Don Juan, Seville's most famous inhabitants.

It would be a mistake to see Seville as merely a city living on myths of toreros, libertines and gypsy flamenco dancers. Seville is – and likes to think of itself as – a thoroughly modern, hard-working city. Twice in the last hundred years (in 1929 and 1992) it has held international exhibitions to convince the world that it is up with the contemporary zeitgeist. While both have left the city with some interesting pieces of architecture, neither has made much impact on traditional Seville. This is a city that will probably leave you guessing what is real and what is cliché.

◆ *The walled gardens of the Reales Alcázares*

When to go

SEASONS & CLIMATE

On 4 August 1881 Seville experienced the highest temperature recorded in Europe: 50°C (122°F). It shouldn't be quite as hot as that when you visit, but this is southern Spain and you can expect it to be anything from agreeably warm to unpleasantly hot. July and August are months best avoided, when the heat drives many residents to decamp to the coast and forces those that stay only to come out in the cool of the evening and night. Even in the thick of winter it rarely gets truly cold, and overcast or rainy days are the exception rather

than the rule. You'd be very unlucky not to be able to have a coffee outdoors on almost any day of the year. Spring is a particularly lovely time to visit because of the blossom and flowers in parks and gardens.

ANNUAL EVENTS

Southern Spain has a busy calendar of traditional fiestas. In Seville the two most important are Holy Week and, immediately after it, the April Fair (see page 12). In May there are spectacular festivals in Córdoba (see page 130), when flower-decked patios are open to the

● *Sevillanos travel in style to the April Fair*

public, and Jerez de la Frontera (see page 110), which stages its Horse Fair. The famous pilgrimage to El Rocío (see below) often also takes place in May although it can be in June. Later on, in even-numbered years (the next is in 2008) Seville stages a flamenco festival in several of the city's auditoriums.

Semana Santa (Holy Week)

Holy Week is celebrated with processions almost everywhere in Spain but nowhere to the extent and extravagance you will see in Seville. During the eight days from Palm Sunday to Easter Sunday 57 brotherhoods carry or push around 100 elaborately decorated *pasos* (floats) in more than 50 processions, many of them in the middle of the night and some of them running concurrently.

The high point is the night of Thursday to Good Friday. The two best processions to see are those of supporters of Seville's 'rival' statues of the Virgin Mary: La Esperanza de Triana and La Esperanza Macarena. More than merely devotional, Seville's Holy Week is an emotional time with people spontaneously shouting *piropos* (compliments) to passing statues of Christ or the Virgin Mary and frequently bursting into songs called *saetas*. Be warned though: Seville gets crowded during Holy Week. Sometimes you can hardly move in the streets, and bars and restaurants are often overflowing.

El Rocío

On Whitsunday (some time between mid-May and mid-June depending on the date of Easter) the little town of El Rocío on the edge of Doñana National Park is swamped by an army of thousands of pilgrims from all over Andalucia. They come to honour the Virgen del Rocío (Virgin of the Dew).

As much as a religious occasion the *romería* (pilgrimage) to El Rocío is a colourful, exuberant affair with many people dressed in Andalucian folk costume. The men wear *traje campero* (short jackets, tight trousers, and leather chaps and boots) and ride horses if they can afford them. The women carry fans and wear vivid polka dot flamenco frills, a flower in their hair or hats and riding boots.

The *de rigueur* way to get to El Rocío is to travel in decorated wagons pulled by oxen or, less romantically these days, by tractor or on horseback. Some stop at night to light a campfire, around which they sing and dance. They make a picturesque sight if you happen to stumble on a party of *rocieros*.

NATIONAL PUBLIC HOLIDAYS
Año Nuevo (New Year's Day) 1 Jan
Día de Reyes (Epiphany) 6 Jan
Andalucia Day 28 Feb
Jueves Santo (Maundy Thursday) Mar/Apr
Viernes Santo (Good Friday) Mar/Apr
Día del Trabajo (Labour Day) 1 May
Día de San Fernando (patron saint of Seville) 30 May
Corpus Christi May/Jun
Virgen de los Reyes (patroness of the city; the Day of the Assumption) 15 Aug
Día de la Hispanidad (Spain's national day) 12 Oct
Todos Los Santos (All Saints' Day) 1 Nov
Día de la Constitución (Constitution Day) 6 Dec
La Inmaculada Concepción (Immaculate Conception) 8 Dec
Día de Navidad (Christmas Day) 25 Dec

The April Fair

Immediately after the excesses of Holy Week, Seville launches into an altogether different type of celebration. There's nothing religious about the April Fair. It's simply an enormous party, six intense days of hyperactivity mainly celebrating Andalucian folk culture. It's held in the fairground in the Barrio de los Remedios. Just follow the tide of people (including women in gaudy flamenco dresses) across the Puente San Telmo from Parque María Luisa or through Triana and you'll find the monumental gateway of lights.

You're welcome to wander around the streets of the fairground and savour the atmosphere, but you'll soon realise that the fair is a combination of private parties taking place in *casetas* (marquees) that are member-only, owned by societies, companies, families and other organisations. What's more, they are often patrolled by security personnel. Fortunately a few *casetas* – notably those owned by political parties – are open to the public and are essentially makeshift bars, which can easily get crowded. Most of the larger *casetas* are equipped with a dance floor. The soundtrack of the fair is the *sevillana*, a home-grown variant of flamenco.

As with all events in Spain, don't arrive too early. By mid-afternoon there is a steady stream of horse-drawn carriages rumbling around the fairground in the Paseo de Caballos and cocky *señoritos* (wearing the typical Andalucian herdsman's outfit of grey, wide-brimmed hat, tight leather breeches and a short jacket) will already be knocking back glasses of *fino* sherry, the fair's preferred tipple.

The music and the dancing get going only in the evening after the bullfight in the Plaza de Toros de la Maestranza (considered an integral part of the fair). It is not just that the fairground is transformed into a spectacle of illuminations by the lanterns, or *farolillos*, along its streets. It's also at night that you are more likely to catch a glimpse of aristocrats, bullfighters, pop stars and other Spanish celebrities drawn by the glamour of the fair.

Seville's fair is undoubtedly the fair to attend, but if you can't make it or you want something less exclusive, try Jerez de la Frontera's fair, which comes shortly after and whose *casetas* are all open to the public.

● *Flamenco finery at the April Fair*

History

Local tradition insists that Hercules, the Greek mythological hero, founded Seville. In reality, though, it was Julius Caesar who, in 45 BC, raised what was probably a small Iberian settlement on the banks of the Guadalquivir to the status of Roman municipality. By the 4th century AD, Hispalis (as it was then known) was one of the most important cities in Spain. But as the Roman Empire crumbled, it was captured by invading hordes of barbarians: first the Vandals, then the Visigoths. Two local clergymen, saints Leander and Isidore, were instrumental in winning the latter away from the Arian heresy and over to mainstream Christianity.

When Muslim (usually known as Moorish) invaders overran Spain from north Africa in 711 they were quick to take the city, which they renamed Isbilya. In the 11th century it became capital of a kingdom that stretched from modern-day Portugal to the east coast of Spain. A fresh wave of Muslim invaders, the Almohads, made Seville their capital, and the city enjoyed another brief moment of splendour of which the famous Giralda tower is the chief reminder.

In 1248 King Fernando III of Castile took Seville for Christianity and made it his residence. The city's mosques were converted into churches. One of his successors, Pedro I, was responsible for building the magnificent royal palace of the Reales Alcázares.

With the fall of Granada in 1492 the Reconquest of Spain was complete. That same year Columbus was dispatched on his historic voyage to the Americas. As a river port close to the Atlantic seaboard, Seville was ideally placed to profit from growing trade with the New World, and the city grew rich on the proceeds.

The good times ended in 1717 when Seville lost its monopoly to nearby Cádiz. The next centuries were hard for the economically struggling city beset by plague and floods. Its woes increased with the loss of Spain's colonies and valuable trade.

In 1929 Seville tried to rebrand itself by staging a Latin American Expo which left little behind except the Parque María Luisa and some elegant architecture. Then came the Spanish Civil War and the depressed postwar era. Seville only recovered with the advent of democracy and a new constitution; widespread devolution meant the city became the capital of Andalucia. Soon after, a local boy, Felipe Gonzalez, became prime minister of Spain.

Since the heady summer of Expo 92 (see below), Seville has been feeling its way in the world, attempting to cling on to its traditions while giving itself a thoroughly modern makeover. A new tramway and light metro system is due to be completed in 2008.

EXPO 92

Expo 92, held from spring to autumn 1992, was visited by around 41 million people. The nominated site on the Isla de la Cartuja was landscaped and transformed by pavilions built by some of the 111 nations participating as well as other supposedly futuristic buildings, some of which have since been put to other uses. Other visible signs of the passing of the Expo are Santa Justa railway station and the high speed AVE (Alta Velocidad Española) rail link with Madrid, an expanded airport and six striking bridges across the river. However, Expo 92 has proved a hard act to live up to. Critics say the money could have been spent on projects of less prestige but more universal use. The piecemeal redevelopment of the Cartuja site seems to at least partly prove their point.

Lifestyle

Sevillanos like to think they are hard-working, but they are also proud of their capacity for going at their own pace and enjoying themselves. The climate imposes a certain rhythm to life and you'll be wise to go with it – particularly in summer when the heat makes it difficult to do anything in a hurry.

A Seville day begins slowly and the morning is long. Lunchtime is late compared with most other countries. Only touristy restaurants start serving before 14.00 and it is not unusual to sit down to a full meal after 15.00.

A long digestive break follows with or without a siesta according to personal preference and the weather. In the summer it makes sense to take a nap in the heat of the day so as to be refreshed and ready to go out when the temperature becomes bearable again in the evening.

The afternoon begins at 16.00–17.00 and many people still have half a working day ahead of them before clocking off at around 21.00.

Dinner is around 22.00–23.00, but is not as heavy as lunch. If the gap between meals becomes interminable, you can always fill it with a few tapas.

To keep up with the locals it's best to adjust to their rhythm and do as they do. Don't try to do everything in one day, give yourself occasional time off, and be prepared for a late night if you want to see the city at its most relaxed.

Although some of the locals can seem brusque at times this is often because they are slightly fazed by dealing with so many tourists who don't speak their language. Most people you meet will be only too helpful. Keep a smile on your face, adopt the local manners and don't be too quick to take offence and you'll get what you want. Particularly important in this gregarious country is to show respect for other people. Always say 'hello' when you enter a shop, bar or any other public place: *buenos días* during the day and *buenas tardes* (good afternoon/evening) from 19.00–20.00 onwards. And don't forget to say *adiós* when you leave.

⬤ *Enjoy a leisurely lunch on the terrace of El Faro de Triana (see page 100)*

Culture

Although Seville is a modern city with a contemporary culture, it takes most of its inspiration from the past and from its tradition. In particular, its greatest creative age was the 17th century, the period of baroque when New World riches paid for art works to furnish palaces, churches and monasteries. One of Spain's greatest painters, Velázquez, was born in Seville although he spent the greater part of his life around the court in Madrid. Much more intimately associated with the city of their birth are the painters Francisco de Zurbarán (1598–1662), Bartolomé Murillo (1617–82) and Juan de Valdés Leal (1662–95), and the sculptor Juan Martínez Montañez (1568–1648). Invariably, given the times in which they lived, these artists were commissioned to portray religious themes but there is great variety in their approaches. While Murillo, for instance, often verges on sentimentality, Zurbarán is widely thought to have brought a sense of spirituality to his work and Valdes Leal's paintings are strikingly expressive and dramatic, executed with a decisive hand and exploiting strong contrasts in colour and shade.

Seville has two other cultural streams of influence that were once looked down on but have recently acquired respectability. One of these is the music and dance of flamenco, which originated as a marginal gypsy form of song and dance but which has now been assimilated into the mainstream and exported all over the world.

The other cultural revival concerns Seville's Muslim (and to some extent Jewish) past. The Christian Reconquest of Spain at the end of the 15th century was meant to be the definitive end of the Moors and their civilisation, and thereafter few people were interested in

▶ *Don Juan, Seville's most famous (or infamous) literary son*

anything not born out of Catholic Christianity. But since the death of Franco (a devout Catholic) and the restoration of democracy, Seville has been busy unearthing and putting on display treasures from its former Muslim self. From time to time there are exhibitions on Al Andalus (Muslim Spain) in venues in Seville, but there are also some permanent reminders that the Christians weren't the only ones with artistic sensibilities. Several churches have strongly suggestive traces in their fabric of the mosques they once were, and one restaurant and one bar occupy parts of separate Moorish baths that have been excavated.

DON JUAN

The fictional character of archetypal, heart-stealing lecher, Don Juan, 'the Trickster of Seville', was dreamt up by priest and playwright Tirso de Molina in the early 17th century. His creation soon acquired a life of its own. Indeed, he stars in subsequent works by Molière, Mozart and George Bernard Shaw among others, and appears in books, films and even a ballet. More than just an unchecked Latin lover, Don Juan is a complex person who has been described as very un-Spanish in the way he destructively pursues his own goals without regard to the norms of society. 'He is hardly a character at all – but a universal day-dream or myth,' wrote VS Pritchett: 'He expresses the male desire for inexhaustible sexual vitality, the female desire to be ravished against the will, reason, interest or honour.'

⏵ *The inner courtyard of the Palacio de la Condesa de Lebrija*

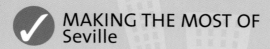

MAKING THE MOST OF
Seville

Shopping

The city's main shopping area centres on two more or less parallel streets, Sierpes and Tetuán/Velázquez, which run from the town hall on Plaza San Francisco and Plaza Nueva north to the squares of La Campana and Plaza Duque de la Victoria. The shops also spread down neighbouring streets towards Plaza de Alfalfa and, in the opposite direction, towards the river. Here you'll find just about everything you'll need: men's and women's fashions, shoes, ceramics and other crafts, jewellery and assorted souvenirs. Seville city centre still has many fascinating smaller, and specialised, shops that haven't yet been driven out by national and international brandname chain stores.

If you don't know where else to look, try El Corte Inglés department store on Plaza Duque de la Victoria or one of the big three shopping centres: Plaza de Armas (closest to the centre, see page 87), Nervión Plaza (see page 87) or Los Arcos (further out, continuing past Nervión Plaza).

⬤ *A hand-painted fan is a wonderful souvenir*

By far the best street market is El Jueves, which is held, as its name says, on Thursdays in the Calle Feria in the Barrio de La Macarena. Principally, it's an antiques market but there are many smaller collectable items for sale and, if nothing else, it's worth attending for the atmosphere.

Craft goods associated with Seville include ceramics (see page 97), *mantones* (shawls, for going out at night or attending the April Fair), lace *mantillas* (traditionally worn during Holy Week and by bridesmaids), *bordados* (embroidery), *encajes* (lacework), fans (often hand-painted), guitars, and flamenco dresses and accessories. Other possible items to take home are bullfighting posters, religious statues, olive oil, wine, sherry and cured Spanish hams.

USEFUL SHOPPING PHRASES

What time do the shops open/close?
¿A qué hora abren/cierran las tiendas?
¿A kay ora abren/theeyerran las teeyendas?

How much is this?
¿Cuánto es?
¿Cwantoe es?

Can I try this on?
¿Puedo probarme esto?
¿Pwedo probarme esto?

My size is ...
Mi número es el ...
Mee noomero es el ...

I'll take this one.
Me llevo éste.
Meh yevo esteh.

This is too large/too small/too expensive.
Do you have any others?
Es muy grande/muy pequeño/muy caro. ¿Tienen más?
Es mooy grandeh/mooy pekenio/mooy karo. ¿Teeyenen mas?

Eating & drinking

Installing yourself in a succession of bars, cafés and restaurants is one of the delights of a visit to Seville. The city has a wide choice of places to eat and drink – from the old-fashioned and quaint, to the vibrantly modern.

The city takes pride in its number and variety of bars and restaurants catering for all tastes and budgets. They go by several different names – including *asador* (indicating that meat is roasted in a wood-fired oven), *mesón* (an antiquated word for an inn),

⬤ *Locals enjoy a drink in El Rinconcillo (see page 88)*

> ## RESTAURANT CATEGORIES
> The price guides given whenever a restaurant is mentioned
> indicate the approximate price of a three-course meal (*menu
> del día* if there is one) for one person, excluding drinks, but
> including tax.
>
> £ = up to €20   ££ = €20–€40   £££ = above €40

cervezería (specialising in beers) and *bodega* or *bodeguita*
(specialising in wines).

For the most part, the cuisine is 'typically Andalucian' – which
means straightforward meat, fish, seafood and vegetable dishes
prepared and served with the minimum of complication and
formality. With such an abundance of good fresh ingredients to
hand there's no need to disguise them with rich sauces. As this is
southern Spain most dishes have olive oil lurking in them
somewhere and dairy foods are used minimally.

If you don't like the local food or want a change from it, the city
has a good choice of restaurants specialising in the cuisines of other
parts of Spain and an array of international restaurants including
Chinese, Japanese, Latin American, Italian and, inevitably, fast food.

The main meal in Spain is eaten in the middle of the day. This is
when most restaurants offer a cheaper menu, *menu del día*, which
typically consists of three courses with a bottle of the house wine
included. This is certainly the best way to fill up without spending
a lot of money. Note that a *menú de degustación* is something
altogether different. Only seen in high-class restaurants, it is a
pricey sampler menu.

Where Seville excels is in its tapas bars, the fast-food joints of
Spain. Even posh restaurants are likely to have a bar attached where

you can eat well without having to order a full meal. Order what you want – if you want a larger portion ask for a *ración* of it – and pay for what you have eaten and drunk at the end. But take care: tapas can easily add up to more than the cost of a *menu del día*. The big thing about tapas is that they are available any time of day or night. You'll never hear anyone in Seville tell you the kitchen is closed and there's nothing to eat!

Tapas are often a godsend to vegetarians visiting Spain. If nothing else, almost every bar can provide a *ración* of meat-free salad or a slice of the old stand-by *tortilla de patata* (potato omelette).

To go with the tapas, Spain has an increasingly good choice of wines, many of them economically priced. Imported bottles, by contrast, are rarely seen and are expensive. If there is a Sevillian drink *par excellence*, it has to be *fino* sherry – a dry fortified wine made in Jerez and drunk chilled.

Spain's main gastronomic failing is its dessert menu, which all too often reduces to a piece of fresh fruit, a scoop of ice cream or the ubiquitous *flan* – crème caramel. But it makes up for this deficiency by being strong on sweet snacks. Seville has several excellent cake shops, *pastelerías*, offering a choice of something to go with a coffee or to fill the long gap between lunch and dinner. The best known of them is La Campana (see page 72).

Another weak point for many visitors – particularly British – is breakfast. Many Spaniards eat hardly anything when they first get up, preferring instead to have a sandwich or snack mid-morning. A few bars do open early and serve a reasonably good breakfast of toast, coffee and fresh orange juice. A popular alternative to this is a portion of *churros* – deep fried sticks of batter that are sprinkled with sugar and dunked into a cup of coffee or hot chocolate.

USEFUL DINING PHRASES

I would like a table for ... people.
Quisiera una mesa para ... personas.
Keyseeyera oona mesa para ... personas.

May I have the bill, please?
¿Podría traerme la cuenta
por favor?
*¿Pordreea trayerme la cwenta
por fabor?*

Waiter/waitress!
¡Camarero/Camarera!
¡Camareroe/Camarera!

Could I have it well-cooked/medium/rare please?
¿Por favor, la carne bien cocida/al punto/roja?
¿Por fabor, la kahrrne beeyen kotheeda/al poontoh/roha?

I am a vegetarian. Does this contain meat?
Soy vegetariano. ¿Tiene carne este plato?
Soy begetahreeahnoh. ¿Teeyene carneh esteh plahtoh?

Where is the toilet (restroom) please?
¿Dónde están los servicios, por favor?
¿Donde estan los serbeetheeos, por fabor?

I would like a cup of/two cups of/another coffee/tea.
Quisiera una taza de/dos tazas de/otra taza de café/té.
*Keyseeyera oona tatha dey/dos tathas dey/otra tatha dey
kafey/tey.*

Entertainment & nightlife

Largely due to the climate but also because of the pattern of the working day, nights out begin late in Seville and go on later – especially in summer when daytime temperatures are too hot to do anything except cower indoors.

● *Ceramic sign for one of the city's flamenco bars*

At any time of year the street life may be enough to entertain you, but there are always regular live-performance venues to draw you in complemented by a busy programme of special events. Everything is listed or advertised in various publications available free from tourist information offices. The best and most complete of them is *El Giradillo* ( www.elgiradillo.es), which is almost entirely in Spanish but still intelligible to a non-speaker.

CINEMA IN ENGLISH

Most films screened in cinemas and on television are dubbed into
Spanish, but you can often see original version (VO) English-
language films (with Spanish subtitles) at Avenida Cines
(ⓐ Marqués de Paradas 15 ❶ 954 29 30 25).

CASINOS

Seville's own casino is the recently inaugurated Gran Casino Aljarafe
(ⓐ Avenida de la Arboleda in Tomares, just outside the city ❶ 902 42
42 22 ⓦ www.grancasinoaljarafe.com). Further away, by the seaside
at Puerto de Santa María, near Cádiz is the Casino Bahía de Cádiz
(❶ 956 87 10 42 ⓦ www.casinobahiadecadiz.es).

THEATRE & CONCERTS

The largest entertainment venue in the city is the El Auditorio
(❶ 954 46 74 08 ⓦ www.auditoriodesevilla.com) on the Isla de la
Cartuja theatre, which stages a diversity of events including most
types of music.

The city's three main theatres (all of which sometimes have
concerts to complement their programmes of plays) are:

Teatro Central ⓐ Isla de la Cartuja ❶ 954 46 08 80
Teatro Lope de Vega ⓐ Avenida María Luisa ❶ 954 59 08 53
Teatro de la Maestranza ⓐ Paseo Colón 22 ❶ 954 22 65 73

Perhaps more interesting is the small, innovative, independent
theatre **Sala La Imperdible** (ⓐ Plaza San Antonio de Padua 9
❶ 954 38 82 19).

NIGHTLIFE

The two golden rules for enjoying the nightlife of Seville are not to
go out too early – certainly not before 23.00 – and not to drink too

much. Many people like to start the evening in one or more *bares de copas*. These are bars for drinking (shorts rather than beers and wines) which don't generally serve tapas. They can be distinguished from everyday bars not only by their late opening hours but also because they have few chairs, not too much light, preened bar staff and loud music on the speakers, possibly controlled by a DJ. Only after midnight or later do people move on to the clubs – although be sure to call them *discotecas* because 'club' in Spanish sometimes has connotations of a roadside brothel.

FLAMENCO

Flamenco is the music, song and dance of Andalucia, particularly of the gypsy community. It is associated especially with the provinces of Seville and Cádiz. The rough wailing voice of the singer is often unaccompanied except by rhythmic clapping, but to this is often added the rapid strumming of a guitar. Songs are never less than full-on passionate and express a range of emotions, mainly sadness and torment. Sometimes the singer and guitarist provide the soundtrack for a dancer – usually female. In true flamenco style, neither the song nor the dance follow a prescribed script. They are never done exactly the same way twice and performers continue for as long as their emotions dictate and stamina allows.

The flamenco shows in Santa Cruz are for tourists but nonetheless good. In Triana it can be more authentic. In Calle Salado you can dance *sevillanas* – pacy folk dances. Purists would say you have to be in the right place at the right time for a spontaneous performance of the real thing.

Sport & relaxation

With its benign climate and abundance of green space, Seville is perfect for watching or taking part in outdoor activities. Its various parks are good places to stroll, run, cycle or Rollerblade. Try, for instance, the green strip beside the river starting near the Puente de Isabel II and continuing beyond the Plaza de Armas shopping centre, and the extensive Parque del Alamillo at the northern end of the Isla de Cartuja.

SPECTATOR SPORTS
Football

The city has two rival teams: FC Sevilla (which plays at the Estadio Ramón Sanchez-Pizjuán ⓐ Luis de Morales ⓣ 902 50 19 01 ⓦ www.sevillafc.es) and Real Betis (which plays at the Estadio Manuel Ruiz de Lopera in Heliopolis, south of the city centre ⓣ 954 61 03 40 ⓦ www.realbetisbalompie.es).

Bullfighting

Newcomers to Spain often don't know what to make of bullfighting, but then many Spaniards don't either. On TV and in the newspapers it's treated as a form of art combining the noblest elements of a spectator sport. Attending a bullfight is respectable almost to the point of being chic. On the other hand, it is easy to condemn *la corrida* as ritualised animal cruelty of the most cynical kind. Perhaps the only thing to do is see a bullfight for yourself and make up your own mind. As Seville has the most famous bullring in the country (see page 80), there is no better place to see what the fuss is about. The season runs from April to October with an important series of bullfights during the April Fair.

⬥ Make up your own mind about Spain's traditional national sport

PARTICIPATION SPORTS
Golf
The 72-par course of the Real Club de Golf de Sevilla (ⓐ Autovía Sevilla-Utrera, Alcalá de Guadaira ❶ 954 12 43 01) is ranked as the third best golf course in Spain and has hosted the WGC World Cup.

RELAXATION
Turkish baths
If you need to unwind, Seville has two Turkish baths. The most conveniently located is Aire de Sevilla (ⓐ Aire 15 ❶ 955 01 00 25 ⓛ 10.00–02.00), which is on an extremely narrow street in the middle of Santa Cruz. Medina al Jarafe (ⓐ Hernán Cortés 12, Bormujos ❶ 954 78 83 44) is on the outskirts of the city. Both have the three traditional rooms of a Turkish bath (*baño arabe* in Spanish) – cold, warm and a 40°C (104°F) hot room – as well as offering a range of massages. Allow 90 minutes for the full treatment.

Accommodation

Seville offers a good choice of places to stay in all price ranges, which is unusual for large Spanish cities.

Hotels are officially ranked from 1 to 5 stars, but this doesn't tell you much except the quantity of facilities. Atmosphere and the standard of service do not always correspond to stars and neither do prices.

Generally cheaper are *hostales* (not to be confused with youth hostels) and *pensiones*. These are guesthouses that usually have en suite rooms but are unlikely to have 24-hour reception or room service and may not offer any meals apart from breakfast.

A well-cared for family-run *pensión* or *hostal* can be a more friendly place to stay and often represents good value for money.

Seville's hotels – including almost all its boutique hotels in converted old houses – are concentrated in the picturesque and touristy Santa Cruz quarter. This means that all the sights – and the best bars and restaurants – are within easy walking distance. That said, you may want to ensure that the place you choose is soundproofed (or at least not near a busy road or a church belfry) and air-conditioned (essential in the summer months).

If you want guaranteed peace and quiet rather than easy access to nightlife, you might be better off staying in a hotel in the

PRICE RATING

The price symbols indicate the approximate price of an en suite room for two people for one night in high season, including tax.

£ = up to €60   **££** = €60–€120   **£££** = above €120

surrounding countryside (e.g. in Carmona – see page 113) and commuting in for sightseeing.

Booking a room is advisable if you are choosy about where you stay and essential in peak holiday periods. For phone bookings you will probably be asked to give a credit card number to confirm the reservation. On arrival you will be asked to show your passport and may have to leave it at reception while the details are copied.

ⓘ Note that accommodation prices can almost double during Holy Week and the April Fair.

🔵 The Hostería del Laurel is in the heart of the Santa Cruz district

HOTELS

Arias £ If you want to be in the city centre and don't mind forgoing a few luxuries in favour of a good price, this may be the place to be. All rooms are en suite with telephone. ❸ Mariana de Pineda ❶ 954 22 68 40 ❿ www.hostalarias.com

Goya £–££ A clean, functional air-conditioned *hostal* in Santa Cruz with 19 rooms equipped with television and phone. ❸ Mateos Gargos 31 ❶ 954 21 11 70 ❿ www.hostalgoyasevilla.com

Sierpes £–££ This *hostal* in Santa Cruz represents a good compromise between price and comforts. The en suite rooms surround a typical Andalucian patio. There is a café and restaurant and, usefully for central Seville, a garage. ❸ Corral del Rey 22 ❶ 954 22 49 48 ❿ www.hsierpes.com

Alcántara ££ A modernised 18th-century mansion with 21 guestrooms in the middle of Santa Cruz. ❸ Ximenez de Enciso 28 ❶ 954 50 06 04 ❿ www.hotelalcantara.net

Amadeus ££ A hotel by and for music lovers occupying an 18th-century house. Each of the individually decorated 14 rooms is named after a composer and concerts are held regularly. Upstairs there is a terrace with views. ❸ Farnesio 6 ❶ 954 50 14 43 ❿ www.hotelamadeussevilla.com

Hostería del Laurel ££ A 22-room hotel and restaurant (see page 74) in one of the picturesque squares at the heart of Santa Cruz. ❸ Plaza de los Venerables 5 ❶ 954 22 02 95 ❿ www.hosteriadellaurel.com

Las Casas del Maestro ££ This house was supposedly built in 1890 by a nobleman for one of his illegitimate children and was later owned by flamenco guitarist Niño Ricardo. All rooms have high ceilings, brass or china door handles and some have four-poster beds.
ⓐ Almudena 5 ⓦ www.lacasadelmaestro.com

Murillo ££ As well as being a hotel named after one of Seville's most famous painters and furnished in an old-fashioned style with armour and antiques, the Murillo also has 14 one- or two-bedroom apartments equipped for self-catering. In the Santa Cruz quarter.
ⓐ Lope de Rueda 9 ⓣ 954 21 60 95 ⓦ www.hotelmurillo.com

Simón ££ An old house with elegance but not too formal in the centre of the city, just west of the cathedral. Suites with sitting rooms and quadruple rooms available. Good value. ⓐ García de Vinuesa 19 ⓣ 954 22 66 60 ⓦ www.hotelsimonsevilla.com

Alcoba del Rey de Sevilla £££ Neo-oriental boutique hotel near the Macarena basilica. The 15 rooms are all different but the bathrooms are particularly lavish. And if you like anything you see in the hotel – even the beds, taps or floors – you can buy it and take it home with you. ⓐ Bécquer 9 ⓣ 954 91 58 00 ⓦ www.alcobadelrey.com

Alfonso XIII £££ The classic luxury hotel of Seville with all the comforts its VIP guests could ask for, including a poolside bar and two restaurants – one of them Japanese (see page 78).
ⓐ San Fernando 2 ⓣ 954 91 70 00 ⓦ www.alfonsoxiii.com

Casa Imperial £££ A converted 16th-century mansion adjacent to the Casa de Pilatos consisting of 24 individually decorated suites, some

with a private terrace. ⓐ Imperial 29 ⓣ 954 50 03 00
ⓦ www.casaimperial.com

Doña María £££ Nowhere else in Seville can you swim or have drinks
and tapas by the poolside while enjoying a view of the cathedral
and Giralda. Each room is dedicated to a famous woman from
Seville's history. ⓐ Don Remondo 19 ⓣ 954 22 49 90
ⓦ www.hdmaria.com

● *Top-class accommodation at the Hotel Alfonso XIII*

Las Casas del Rey de Baeza £££ An 18th-century mansion standing on a cobbled square, with a classical façade and a peaceful courtyard. Spacious bedrooms. Good breakfast. There's a small open air pool on the roof. ⓐ Plaza Jesús de la Redención 2 ⓣ 954 56 14 96 ⓦ www.hospes.es

Taberna del Alabardero £££ This hotel occupies the sensitively restored 19th-century house of a renowned Seville poet. It has seven comfortable rooms named after the provinces of Andalucia. Better known as a restaurant (see page 90). ⓐ Zaragoza 20 ⓣ 954 50 27 21 ⓦ www.tabernadelalabardero.com

YOUTH HOSTELS

Oasis Backpackers Hostel £ Claims always to have space for walk-in guests. Breakfast is included in the price. ⓐ Calle Alonso el Sabio 1A ⓣ 954 29 37 77 ⓦ www.oasissevilla.com

Sevilla Youth Hostel £ The city's official (Hostelling International) youth hostel with a capacity of 277 guests is 1.5 km (1 mile) from the city centre next to the campus of Reina Mercedes University. ⓐ Isaac Peral 2 ⓣ 955 05 65 00

CAMPSITES

The three closest campsites to Seville are as follows.

Camping Club de Campo ⓐ en Autovía Sevilla-Cadiz, Dos Hermanas ⓣ 954 72 02 50
Camping Oromana ⓐ Camino del Maestre, Alcalá de Guadaira ⓣ 955 68 32 57 ⓦ www.campingoromana.es
Camping Villsom ⓐ Dos Hermanas ⓣ 954 72 08 28

THE BEST OF SEVILLE

Whether you are on a flying visit to Seville or taking a more leisurely break in southern Spain, here are some of the sights and activities you should try not to miss.

TOP 10 ATTRACTIONS

- **Barrio de Santa Cruz** A picture-postcard-pretty complex of streets and squares (see page 60).

- **Cathedral and La Giralda** Two sights in one. The Giralda is essentially a topped-up minaret with a ramp leading all the way to the top. The tower makes a handy landmark to get your bearings. The massive Gothic cathedral below contains the tomb of Christopher Columbus (see page 65).

- **Spring Fiestas** Two very different celebrations fall close together, both of them spectacular. First come the processions of Holy Week (see page 10). Shortly afterwards comes the exuberant April Fair (see page 12).

- **Flamenco** The emblematic music and dance of southern Spain comes in many forms but is always performed with passion. There are plenty of places where you can see a show. And there is a museum to explain it (see page 69).

- **Museo de Bellas Artes** One of the great art galleries of Spain concentrating on Seville's 'Golden Age' painters (see page 85).

- **Plaza de España** An extravagantly tiled monument in celebration of Spain in all its facets, this is the most prominent building in the leafy Parque de María Luisa, former showground of an international exhibition (see page 80).

- **Plaza de Toros de la Real Maestranza** The most famous bullring in the world. It's best to see it when packed out for a top *corrida*, but you can take a guided tour of it at any time (see page 80).

- **Reales Alcázares** An exquisite royal palace built by the Christian kings of Castile in glorious Moorish style. The oldest occupied royal palace in Europe. It also has beautiful gardens (see page 67).

- **Río Guadalquivir** Seville wouldn't be Seville without its river, which is crossed by nine bridges. You can take a trip down it, stroll along its banks, or sit on a terrace of a bar or restaurant and take in a view of it at your leisure (see page 58).

- **Torre del Oro** There's not much to the short little 'Golden Tower' on the river bank, but it's still a Seville landmark (see page 82).

◗ *Magnificent tiled entrance to the Monasterio de Santa María de las Cuevas (see page 98)*

Your brief guide to seeing and experiencing the best of Seville, depending on the time you have available.

HALF DAY: SEVILLE IN A HURRY

If you have only a morning or afternoon in Seville, there's no choice to make. Spend it in the Barrio de Santa Cruz, but go up the Giralda tower as well. If you're quick, you may be able to get around the Reales Alcázares, next door to the cathedral, as well. Santa Cruz has innumerable tapas bars and restaurants where you can grab a bite to eat to begin or end your visit.

1 DAY: TIME TO SEE A LITTLE MORE

With a whole day in Seville your best option is to stay in Santa Cruz and see the Cathedral, the Giralda and the Reales Alcazáres at your leisure. You should also be able to stroll down to the riverside and see the Torre del Oro and bullring.

2–3 DAYS: SHORT CITY-BREAK

One day will be spent as above, but the extra days will give you a chance to do more. Depending on your interest, you may choose to visit Triana, the Museo de Bellas Artes or the Parque de María Luisa. You could also take a day trip out of the city, perhaps to see Doñana National Park or even Córdoba.

LONGER: ENJOYING SEVILLE TO THE FULL

With a week or more you'll have time to fit in everything you want to see and do. If this is your first visit to southern Spain, try to get over to Granada for a day or two. You may want to spend another couple of days exploring Ronda and the White Towns.

NO8DO

Almost everywhere you go in Seville you'll see a symbol like some slick, inscrutable brand name carved on walls and written on posters: NO8DO.

Rather than a modern commercial invention it is a civic insignia that has been in use since the 13th century. Traditionally – and no one has yet come up with a better theory – it is held to be a mark of gratitude from King Alfonso X the Wise to the city for staying loyal to him during a struggle for the succession. It almost needs a competent texter to interpret it. The '8' stands for a skein of wool or *madeja* and so the message reads: *No-madeja-do* or *no me ha dejado* – that is, 'She [Seville] hasn't abandoned me.'

Something for nothing

To see the best of Seville you don't have to spend money. You can enjoy its charm simply by strolling around its streets, squares and gardens. The Santa Cruz quarter is the obvious place to spend most time, but window shopping in the city centre also has its interest. If you've got time on your hands but no cash in your pockets, other good places to walk and see sights for free are the riverbanks and bridges of the Guadalquivir, Parque de María Luisa (especially the Plaza de España) and the former Expo 92 grounds on the Isla de Cartuja, which have a sort of postmodern fascination.

Plan ahead and you can see many of the city's essential monuments and museums without parting with a penny. Some of those that are not free all the time have a particular day of the week on which they waive the admission charge. The Archivo de Indias, Basílica de la Macarena and Hotel Alfonso XIII are free all the time to everyone. The Museo de Bellas Artes and the archaeological museum are free to citizens of EU countries. The Centro Andaluz de Arte Contemporáneo on the Isla de Cartuja is free to EU citizens on Tuesdays (its grounds are free at any time), and the Torre del Oro and the Casa de Pilatos (afternoon only) are also free that day. The cathedral and Hospital de los Venerables are free on Sundays.

If you do your research well, you can turn the situation to your advantage and go in search of sights that other visitors might not bother with. La Macarena has several old churches, for instance, with vestiges of the mosques over which they were built. The Plaza de Armas shopping centre is the handsome old engine shed of a former railway station. Even in the middle of much transited Santa Cruz are three neglected Roman columns, immensely tall and rising out of a lush green pit in the ground on Calle Mármoles.

If you happen to be in Seville in spring, you will have all the street entertainment you want for free: first the semi-solemn semi-jubilant processions of Holy Week; then the troops of gaudily dressed women heading on foot and in horse-drawn carriage for the showground of the April Fair.

🔺 *Enjoy a stroll in the Parque de María Luisa*

When it rains

In summer, you'll probably be grateful for a little rain to cool things down. But at any other time of year, a few wet days can dampen your expectations of seeing a city in which sunshine and blue skies are the norm. Seville just isn't the same under brooding skies and it is as well to have a back-up plan to turn a disadvantage into a positive.

The obvious thing to do is take refuge in a museum such as the Museo de Bellas Artes, flamenco museum, archaeological museum or Palacio de la Condesa de Lebrija. Similarly, the Archivo de Indias and cathedral (but not the Giralda tower) are also places you can get the best out of whatever the weather is doing. The Casa de Pilatos, Reales Alcázares and Centro Andaluz de Arte Contemporáneo offer at least something on a rainy day, although you won't see their outdoor spaces at their best.

Alternatively, you could forget sightseeing altogether and get down to some serious shopping. If you don't want to get wet hopping between shops it may be best to confine yourself to a department store such as El Corte Inglés (see page 71) or a shopping centre where you can keep dry as long as your money holds out. All have a good choice of bars and restaurants in which you can prolong your visit. The Plaza de Armas (see page 87) is the city's most convenient and pleasant shopping centre, but you may want somewhere larger – in which case head for Nervión Plaza (see page 87) which has a cinema next to it, or, further still, Los Arcos.

Another option is to find yourself a pleasant bar (not hard to do in Seville) and either strike up a conversation with the locals or sit out the showers with a good book.

If you prefer to indulge yourself with physical pleasure while it pours down outside you can retreat into one of the city's Turkish baths (see page 33).

On a rainy evening when you feel like going out, try one of the flamenco shows in Santa Cruz or El Arenal.

🔺 *The Archivo General de Indias is a good bet if you're unlucky enough to get rain*

On arrival

Most visitors to Seville arrive at either the airport (a bus or taxi ride from the centre) or the railway station (just within walking distance). Either way, unless you already have a hotel to go to, the best thing to do is get as close to the cathedral marked by the distinctive Giralda tower and find your bearings there.

TIME DIFFERENCES

Spain follows Central European Time (CET). From late March to late September the clocks are put ahead 1 hour. In the Spanish summer, at 12.00 noon, time at home is as follows.

Australia Eastern Standard Time 20.00, Central Standard Time 19.30, Western Standard Time 18.00
South Africa 12.00
New Zealand 22.00
UK 11.00
USA and Canada Newfoundland Time 07.30, Atlantic Canada Time 07.00, Eastern Time 06.00, Central Time 05.00, Mountain Time 04.00, Pacific Time 03.00, Alaska 02.00

ARRIVING
By air

National and international flights arrive at San Pablo airport, 12 km (7.5 miles) east of the city on the road to Córdoba and Madrid ⊕ 954 44 90 00 ⓦ www.aena.es

The quickest way to get into the city, depending on the traffic, is to take a taxi from an official rank. Buses between the city centre and the airport run from approximately 06.15 to 11.00.

By rail

Seville's principal railway station is Santa Justa on Avenida de Kansas City (❶ 954 41 41 11), about 20 minutes' walk east of the city centre (or a short bus ride). High speed AVE trains from Madrid arrive here (❶ 954 54 03 03) as well as trains from cities closer by including Jerez, Cádiz and Córdoba. There is another much smaller railway station, San Bernardo, in front of the Hospital Virgen del Rocío. Spain's main rail operator is Renfe. ❶ 902 24 02 02

By coach

If you arrive by coach you will be dropped off at one of the city's two bus stations:

Plaza de Armas ❶ 954 90 77 37 (services mainly from western Spain and Madrid)

🔺 *Seville's main railway station, Santa Justa*

Prado de San Sebastián ⓐ Manuel Vázquez Sagastizábal ❶ 954 41 71 11 (from other destinations)

Driving

If you have to drive into Seville, it's best to have a secure parking place lined up and head straight for it. Avoid rush hour and driving in the twisting streets of Santa Cruz and La Macarena. If there is a quieter time to be driving in the city it is during the lunch break, around 15.00–16.00.

FINDING YOUR FEET

Seville is a lively, busy city and inevitably, like any big city, it has its criminals on the lookout for easy prey. That said, you should have no problems if you always keep your bag and camera close to you and don't stop in a dark alley to look at your map.

ORIENTATION

It's worth spending your first hour or so in the city becoming familiar with the layout, especially before you plunge into the labyrinthine streets of the Santa Cruz quarter. The cathedral and its Giralda tower are always the main point of reference, and the river means you can never stray too far to the west.

❶ Note that many maps of Seville show the river running horizontally across them with east at the top, not north.

GETTING AROUND

In most cases you can forget about buses and taxis. The best way to get from sight to sight is to walk. Certainly, in Santa Cruz you have no other option to the further points of the Parque de María Luisa and to the Isla de la Cartuja. But one of the great pleasures of Seville is to wander without haste, discovering little-known bars and shops on your way. The city is full of details – particularly ceramic murals – that not even some of the locals notice.

Local bus

Bus services are efficient except when the traffic snarls up during rush hours or because of works on Seville's forthcoming light railway and tram system. You can pay the driver for each journey on boarding or buy a card valid for ten journeys from *estancos* (tobacconists, marked 'Tabac'). There are also three- and seven-day passes available. The most useful route is C4, which circles round

IF YOU GET LOST, TRY ...

Excuse me, do you speak English?
¿Perdone, habla usted inglés?
¿Perdoene, ahbla oosteth eengless?

Excuse me, is this the right way to the old town/the city centre/the tourist office/the station/the bus station?
¿Perdone, por aquí se va a el casco antiguo/al centro de la ciudad/oficina de turísmo/la estación de trenes/estación de autobuses?
¿Perdoneh, porr akee seh bah ah el kasko antigwo/al thentroe de la theeoodath/offeetheena deh toorismoe/la estatheeon de trenes/estatheeon dey awtoebooses?

Can you point to it on my map?
¿Puede señalármelo en el mapa?
¿Pwede senyarlarmeloe en el mapa?

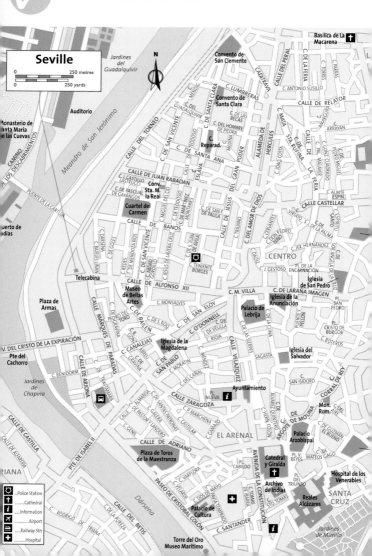

Seville

0 ———— 250 metres
0 ———— 250 yards

Basilica de La Macarena

Convento de San Clemente

Jardines del Guadalquivir

N

Auditorio

Convento de Santa Clara

Monasterio de Santa Maria de las Cuevas

C. DEL TORNEO

CALLE DE LA FERIA

CALLE DEL PERAL

C. DE LAS TORRES

C. PAÑAS

C. ANTONIO SUSILLO

CALLE DE RELATOR

CALATRAVA

C. LUMBRERAS

C. DE SANTA CLARA

C. DEL GUADALQUIVIR

C. DE LAS BECAS

C. DEL HOMBRE DE PIEDRA

C. MAYA

STA. RUFINA

CALLE CASTELLAR

C. DE SAN VICENTE

C. DE SAN VICENTE

C. DE TEODOSIO

C. Reparad.

C. DE SANTA ANA

ALAMEDA DE HÉRCULES

C. DEL GRAN PODER

C. DE LA FERIA

CAMINO DE LOS DESCUBRIMIENTOS

PUENTE DE LA CARTUJA

CALLE DE JUAN RABADAN

C. I. CASTILLO LASTRUCCI

Conv. Sta. M. la Real

C. DE PASCUAL DE GAYANGOS

Cuartel del Carmen

CALLE DE BAÑOS

DE

MIGUEL DEL CID

C. TELODODDO

C. MARTINEZ MONTAÑES

C. DE SAN LUIS DE PAULA

C. DE JESÚS

C. DEL AMOR DE DIOS

C. TRAJANO

Puerto de Indias

Telecabina

Plaza de Armas

C. DARSENA

C. BAILÉS JUAN

C. REYES

C. DE MENDOZA RÍOS

C. CARDENAL CISNEROS

CABELLO GORDILLO

C. TENIENTE BORGES

C. JESÚS DEL GRAN PODER

CENTRO

CALLE DE ALFONSO XII

C. M. VILLA

J. GESTOSO

PL. DE LA ENCARNACIÓN

Iglesia de San Pedro

Museo de Bellas Artes

C. DE SAN VICENTE

C. MONSALVES

C. DE S. ROQ.

C. DE SAN ELOY

C. DE LARANA

IMAGEN

PL. SAN PEDRO

Iglesia de la Anunciación

Palacio de Lebrija

C. DE LA CUNA

PUENTE Y PELLÓN

PL. CRISTO DE BURGOS

C. BOTEROS

V. DEL CRISTO DE LA EXPIRACIÓN

CALLE MÁRQUES DE PARADAS

Pte del Cachorro

Jardines de Chapina

CALLE DE ARJONA

C. CANALEJAS

C. DE GRAVINA

Iglesia de la Magdalena

C. SAN PABLO

C. O'DONNELL

C. DE VELILLA

C. RIOJA

CALLE VELÁZQUEZ

SAGASTA

Iglesia del Salvador

SAN ISIDORO

CORRAL DEL REY

Mon. Rom.

CALLE DE CASTILLA

CALLE ALVAREZ

TRIANA

PTE DE ISABEL II

C. BENIDORM

Plaza de Toros de la Maestranza

CALLE DE ADRIANO

Plaza de Cultura

PASEO DE CRISTÓBAL COLÓN

EL ARENAL

Ayuntamiento

PL. NUEVA

CALLE ZARAGOZA

C. R. MARCHENA

ARGOTE DE MOLINA

Palacio Arzobispal

Catedral y Giralda

Archivo de Indias

PL. DEL TRIUNFO

Reales Alcázares

Hospital de los Venerables

SANTA CRUZ

AVENIDA DE LA CONSTITUCIÓN

Palacio de Cultura

Torre del Oro Museo Marítimo

Dársena

CALLE DEL BETIS

C. RODRIGO DE TRIANA

Jardines de Murillo

Legend
- Police Station
- Cathedral
- Information
- Airport
- Railway Stn
- Hospital

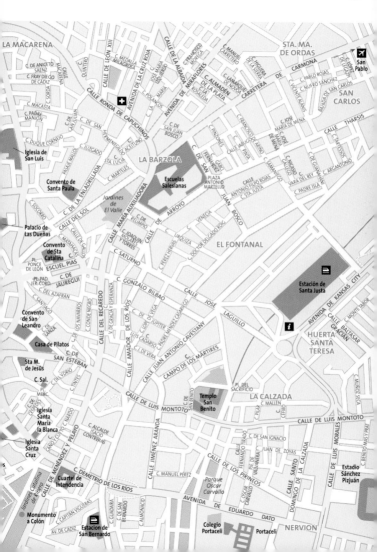

the city centre. There is a concentration of bus stops around the Puerta de Jerez at the end of Avenida Constitución.

☎ 900 85 55 58 **Ⓦ** www.consorciotransportes-sevilla.com

Metro

A previous attempt to construct a metro system was abandoned in the 1970s because of fears of damage to historic buildings. However, in 1999, a new project was started. The metro system is currently under construction and due to open sometime in 2007.

Tour buses

A good way to see a lot in a hurry is to take an open-top double-decker tour bus ride. Although these are advertised as hop on, hop off services there are only actually four stops. However, their great advantage is that they enable you to skim through the two fair grounds (1929 and 1992), which aren't as rewarding to visit on foot. The place to pick up these buses is near the Torre del Oro.

SevillaTour **☎** 902 10 10 81 **Ⓦ** www.sevillatour.com

Sevirama Tour por Sevilla **☎** 954 56 06 93 **Ⓦ** www.busturistico.com

Taxis

Taxis are easily hailed on any main street and not too costly. But for many journeys in central Seville – particularly in Santa Cruz – it is quicker (and more enjoyable) to walk. For a pick up call **Radio Taxi** **☎** 954 58 00 00 or **Tele Taxi** **☎** 954 62 22 22.

❶ A green light means a taxi is for hire. The fare will be fixed by meter, which may start at a minimum charge. Tariffs increase at night and if you have luggage.

Car

Narrow streets and traffic jams mean it's not worth trying to drive around the city centre. In addition, car parks and parking spaces can be hard to find. If you have arrived by car it is best to leave it parked in a hotel garage or secure car park and explore on foot, public transport or taxi. For information on car hire, see page 144.

Bicycle hire

With no hills, Seville is a good city to cycle around. What's more, there are a few dedicated cycle lanes, including a recreational one beside the river near the Plaza de Armas shopping centre. A bicycle

● *Take a taxi from the station – otherwise, it's more fun to walk*

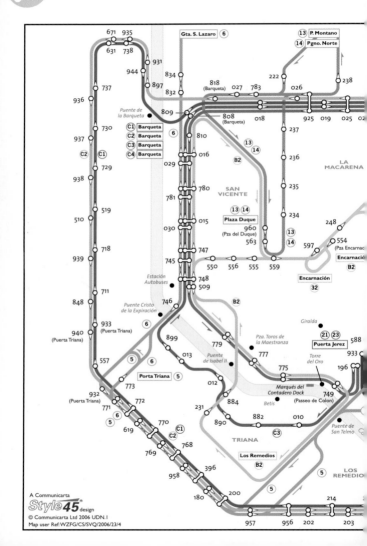

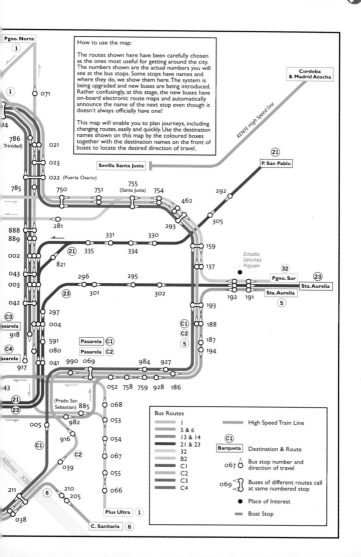

How to use the map:

The routes shown here have been carefully chosen as the ones most useful for getting around the city. The numbers shown are the actual numbers you will see at the bus stops. Some stops have names and where they do, we show them here. The system is being upgraded and new buses are being introduced. Rather confusingly, at this stage, the new buses have on-board electronic route maps and automatically announce the name of the next stop even though it doesn't always officially have one!

This map will enable you to plan journeys, including changing routes, easily and quickly. Use the destination names shown on this map by the coloured boxes together with the destination names on the front of buses to locate the desired direction of travel.

Pgno. Norte
①
①
071
786 Trinidad
021
023
022 (Puerta Osario)
785
750   751   755 (Santa Justa)   754
281
888
889
002
043
003
042
©3 Pasarela
918
©4 Pasarela
917
297
004
591
080
041   990   069   984   927
052   758   759   928   186
43
②1
②3
(Prado San Sebastian) 885   068
005
982
916   053
©1
©2   067
039
211   210   055
205
038   066
6

331   330
335   334
821
296   295
301   302
293
292
462
305
159
137
Estadio Sánchez Pizjuán
192   191
193
©1
©2   188
5   187
194

Sevilla Santa Justa

Cordoba & Madrid Atocha

RENFE High Speed line

②1 P. San Pablo

32
Pgno. Sur   ②3
Sta. Aurelia
Sta. Aurelia
5

Pasarela ©1
Pasarela ©2

Plus Ultra ①
C. Sanitaria ⑥

Bus Routes
— 1
— 5 & 6
— 13 & 14
— 21 & 23
— 32
— B2
— C1
— C2
— C3
— C4

— High Speed Train Line

©1 Barqueta   Destination & Route

067 Ⓞ   Bus stop number and direction of travel

069   Buses of different routes call at same numbered stop

● Place of Interest

— Boat Stop

Alfonso XIII

can be a good way of exploring the far reaches of the Parque de María Luisa and the Isla de la Cartuja, but it's almost impossible to avoid busy roads. For bicycle hire contact Cyclotour at either Avenida de Hernán Cortés in Parque de María Luisa or Paseo Marqués de Contadero (next to the Torre del Oro) ❶ 954 27 45 66 ⓦ www.cyclotouristic.com

River cruises

Seville looks different from the river as the traffic noise recedes and you sail under its various bridges. Cruises are operated by Cruceros Torre del Oro (ⓐ Alcalde Marqués de Contadero, next to the Torre del Oro ❶ 954 56 16 92 ⓦ www.crucerostorredeloro.com). Boats leave every 30 minutes 10.00–22.00 for a 1-hour trip to see the historical and modern sights of the city. At weekends from May to September they also sail down to the mouth of the Guadalquivir at Sanlúcar de Barrameda on the edge of Doñana National Park (see page 108).

HORSE-DRAWN CARRIAGES

These exist, of course, purely for tourists but, come the April Fair, anyone who is anyone in Seville will be seen driving around Seville at horse-pace. And it is an undeniably leisurely and enjoyable way to get the flavour of the city.

ⓐ Drivers wait for fares in the Plaza del Triunfo outside the cathedral, in the Parque de María Luisa (next to the Plaza de España) and near the Torre del Oro.

● *The Torre del Oro is one of the city's most famous landmarks*

Santa Cruz & the city centre

If Seville thinks it is the centre of Andalucia, then the **Barrio de Santa Cruz** is sure that it is the heart and soul of Seville. And indeed if all the allures of southern Spain could be distilled into one neighbourhood of one city, this tangle of picturesque streets, squares and beguiling alleyways would be it.

Despite the waves of tourists that parade through it every day and the increasing gentrification of the area, Santa Cruz has lost none of its flavour and is a seamless blend of the authentic and the stereotypical: white houses with details picked out in ochre and crimson, the forbidding iron grilles over their windows offset by pots of flowering geraniums. It's no cliché that the air is perfumed with orange blossom and the fragrance of jasmine. At every turn, it seems, there is some pleasant bar or restaurant with outdoor tables ready for breakfast, tapas or a leisurely meal. And a great many of Santa Cruz's mansions built around secretive patios have been turned into boutique hotels.

Chiefly what has preserved Santa Cruz intact is that there are few streets through it built for cars. Some streets are so narrow that two people can hardly pass without turning sideways. In fact, one street is known locally as 'the street of the kiss' because two lovers leaning out of windows on either side could smooch across it.

The best but busiest pedestrian route into Santa Cruz is through the short tunnel in the corner of Patio de Banderas (next to the exit from the Reales Alcázares) which leads you into Calle Judería, whose name is a reminder that this was the Jewish quarter of the city until the Jews were expelled from Spain in 1492.

Santa Cruz proper stretches east from here to Calle Menéndez y Pelayo – this is its picture-postcard core – but it continues

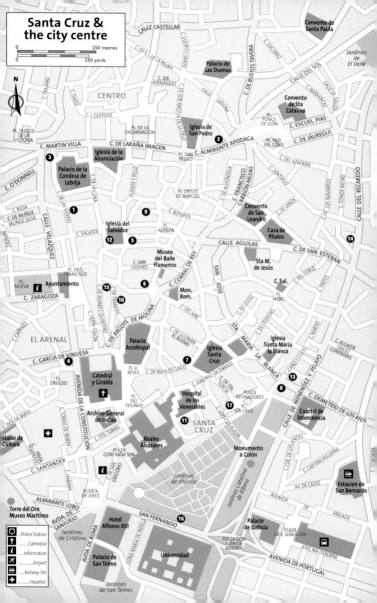

northwards to the Casa de Pilatos with streets and squares that are not quite so perfect but where tourists and locals are more evenly balanced.

Once immersed in the labyrinth, a map is not much use; the only thing to do is navigate by nose, but there are sometimes two landmarks to help you. Occasionally you'll catch a glimpse of the Giralda, giving you a rough west point; to the south the barrio is limited by the gardens of the Reales Alcázares and next to them the Jardines de Murillo.

Beautiful though it is, after a while Santa Cruz can feel a little claustrophobic. So it can be a relief to discover Seville's agreeable city centre, helpfully known simply as 'Centro'. Here Seville's best shops are concentrated along Calle Sierpes and Tetuán/Velázquez, which run between Plaza Nueva/Plaza San Francisco and Plaza Campana/Plaza del Duque de la Victoria.

SIGHTS & ATTRACTIONS

Casa de Pilatos

This aristocratic palace dates from the late 15th and early 16th centuries and speaks of Seville at its most wealthy and powerful. It was named 'the House of Pontius Pilate' after one of its early owners, Don Fadrique, the first Marquis of Tarifa, returned from the Holy Land in 1519 and discovered that the distance between it and a local shrine was the same as that between the supposed site of the Praetorium (where Christ was condemned to death) in Jerusalem and Golgotha (where he was crucified). Struck by this coincidence, the Marquis laid out a series of Stations of the Cross starting from the house and the processions between them that took place in his day are thought to have given rise to Seville's famous Holy Week celebrations.

The house, owned by the Dukes of Medinaceli and administered on their behalf by a foundation, is in a mixture of Gothic, Mudejar (derived from Islamic architecture) and Italian Renaissance styles. It has a number of interesting decorative features including coffered ceilings, paintings, furniture, classical statues, frescoes and a marvellous dome over the main staircase. The walls around the two-storey central patio are worth seeing (even if you ignore the rest of the building), as they are covered with old tiles in a glorious clash of colours and styles. Outside, the Renaissance gardens are worth seeing too.

ⓐ Plaza de Pilatos 1 ⓣ 954 22 52 98 ⓛ 09.00–18.00 Jan & Feb, Sept–Dec; 09.00–19.00 Mar–Aug. Free on Tues 13.00–17.00

⬤ *The tranquil, shady gardens of the Casa de Pilatos*

Catedral y Giralda

'We'll build a church that will make anyone who looks at it think we were mad,' the city fathers are supposed to have said in the early 14th century as they set out to build Seville's great cathedral. The building took over a century to complete and the result was, and is, the largest Gothic building in Europe and the third largest church in Christendom after St Peter's in Rome and St Paul's in London. It dominates the city centre forming a block of its own delineated by steps and chains, its façades facing the four cardinal points.

● *The Giralda tower soars over Seville's massive Gothic cathedral*

It stands on the site of a 12th-century mosque built by the Almohad civilisation that ruled southern Spain at the time. The only surviving remains of the original building are the cloister of the Patio de los Naranjos ('Courtyard of the Orange Trees', which was used for ritual ablutions by Muslim worshippers) and the Giralda tower, formerly a minaret, which looms above the cathedral as the city's unmistakable landmark.

Inside, five aisles divided into nine sections each, and flanked by 20 chapels, create a massive floor space. The focal point is inevitably the high altar with its great altarpiece, one of the largest in the world, made of gold panels carved in relief by Flemish and Spanish artists.

WHO'S IN CHRISTOPHER COLUMBUS'S TOMB?

Columbus died in Valladolid on 20 May 1506 and was initially buried in a cemetery in the city. Three years later his family had the corpse taken to Seville where his eldest son, Diego, was buried beside him in 1526. But Diego's widow insisted on having both bodies moved to Santo Domingo on the Caribbean island of Hispaniola. When the French threatened to capture Hispaniola in 1795, a worried Spain had his remains transferred for safe keeping to Havana, Cuba. A century later, Cuba gained its independence and Columbus was moved to his final resting place in Seville cathedral. Or was he?

With each move came the possibility of a mistake being made and there is evidence that the body of Diego (rather than that of his father) was mistakenly moved to Cuba. This would mean that Christopher Columbus lies buried in Santo Domingo in the Dominican Republic rather than under the grand sepulchre built for him in the cathedral of Seville.

Other features to look out for are the Royal Chapel, the 138 stained glass windows and the ornate tomb of Christopher Columbus.

The highlight of the visit, however, is a walk up the 104-m (341-ft) high Giralda tower. The tower has a series of ramps running up the middle of it which once allowed horses or mules to be ridden to the top. These days, there are a few steps to negotiate at the top.

The tower is actually an ingenious bit of architectural grafting as it is one tower superimposed on another. The bottom two-thirds are

● *Moorish designs in the courtyard of the Reales Alcázares*

a brick-built minaret; the upper part is a stone-and-brick Renaissance belfry added in 1568. On the pinnacle of the spire stands a weathervane: a bronze figure of Faith popularly known as 'El Giraldillo' from which the tower derives its name.

❸ Plaza Virgen de los Reyes (Puerta del Lagarto) ❶ 954 21 49 71 ⓦ www.catedralsevilla.org ⓛ 11.00–18.00 Mon–Sat, Sept–June; 09.30–15.30 Mon–Sat, Jul & Aug; 14.30–19.00 Sun. Free on Sun

Hospital de los Venerables

This residence for old or ill priests ('venerable gentlemen') was built in 1675 and is now a cultural centre used for exhibitions. It's church is a masterpiece of Sevillian baroque decoration and painting. See particularly the *trompe l'oeil* of the *Triumph of the Cross* by Juan de Valdés Leal on the sacristy ceiling with its angels floating in mid-air.

❸ Plaza de los Venerables ❶ 954 56 26 96 ⓦ www.focus.abengoa.es ⓛ 10.00–14.00, 16.00–20.00. Free Sun pm

Reales Alcázares

When the King of Spain visits Seville, this is where he stays, giving the Alcázar its claim to be the oldest occupied royal palace in Europe. It's also the first and finest civil building in the city and deserving of a lengthy visit.

Really, it's a series of palaces, a successive amplification of an original governor's palace built in 913 or 914. What makes it special is the way in which Muslim architectural styles have been fused with Christians ones (Gothic, Renaissance). But in particular it is considered one of the foremost treasures of Mudejar art, a singularly Spanish medieval style created by Muslim craftsmen employed by Christian rulers.

The core of the Alcazar is the Mudejar Palace (also called the Palacio de Don Pedro), which was created by Pedro I (the Cruel)

between 1364 and 1366. To fulfil his plans he sent to Córdoba and Granada for the best Muslim craftsmen working in his day.

The complex is entered by the Puerta del León, which leads into the Patio del León. One room to the left is the Patio del Yeso (Patio of the Plaster), the only bit of the Almohad palace still intact.

From the Patio del León you step into the Patio de la Montería, the fulcrum of the complex where the court used to assemble for hunting expeditions. Directly in front of you is the façade of the Mudejar Palace. But before you enter it, have a look at the audience chamber, or Casa de Contratación, to the right. Against one wall here is the *Altarpiece of the Navigators*, painted in 1531–6 and almost certainly the first work of art to depict the discovery of the Americas. In its central panel the Virgin Mary spreads her cape protectively over an assembly of discoverers and conquistadores, including Columbus and Hernán Cortés. Below them are various ships of the period.

The finest room of the palace is the Salón de los Embajadores (Hall of the Ambassadors), which is noticeable for its horseshoe arches, tiles and intricate plasterwork and, most of all, its great dome – a complex geometric arrangement of interlocking gold-painted wood.

Also worth seeing are the Patio de las Muñecas (Patio of the Dolls) named after the two small faces that adorn one of its arches, and the Patio de las Doncellas (Patio of the Maidens), with its superb plasterwork.

North of the Mudejar Palace you pass into the Salones de Carlos V, sumptuous, Gothic-vaulted apartments and a chapel added on the orders of the eponymous monarch.

Behind the palace is a large triangle of walled gardens, a delightful combination of old and new landscaping displaying both English and Arab–Andalucian influences in its combinations of terraces, ponds, fountains, monuments, gateways and bowers.

ⓐ Patio de Banderas ☎ 954 50 23 23 ⓦ www.patronato-alcazarsevilla.es ⏰ 09.30–19.00 Tues–Sat, 09.30–17.00 Sun, Apr–Sept; 09.30–17.00 Tues–Sat, 09.30–13.30 Sun, Oct–Mar. Admission charge

CULTURE

Archivo General de Indias

This immense depository of the records of imperial Spain's centuries of colonialism occupies a 16th-century building, which began life as a commercial exchange for the merchants of the city. In the 18th century King Carlos III decided to use it to archive in one place the vast store of documents relating to Spain's New World possessions. It is still a working library consulted by scholars from all over the world. Its 8 km (5 miles) of shelves hold 43,000 files and more than 80 million pages of original documents – including Columbus's journal, and letters written by Hernán Cortés and Miguel de Cervantes, author of *Don Quixote*.

ⓐ Avenida de la Constitución ☎ 954 21 12 34
ⓦ www.mcu.es/archivos/visitas/index.html. Free

Museo del Baile Flamenco

This recently opened museum aims to present flamenco as a mainstream art form. There's a gift shop selling various flamenco-related items, plus evening concerts. If you are here for long enough, you can even take flamenco dance classes.

ⓐ Calle Manuel Rojas Marcos 3, near Plaza Alfalfa ☎ 954 34 03 11
ⓦ www.museoflamenco.com ⏰ 09.00–18.00 (09.00–19.00 in summer)

Palacio de la Condesa de Lebrija

This 16th-century Renaissance–Mudejar palace could be considered the city's alternative archaeological museum. Among many other items is one of the finest mosaics from the Roman remains of Itálica (see page 104). Upstairs are the living quarters of the eponymous countess.

ⓐ Cuna 8 ⓣ 954 22 78 02 ⓦ www.palaciodelebrija.com
ⓛ 10.30–13.30, 17.00–20.00 Mon–Fri, 10.00–14.00 Sat

RETAIL THERAPY

Adolfo Domínguez Spanish designer known especially for his men's suits and shoes. ⓐ Sierpes 2 ⓛ 10.15–14.00, 17.00–20.30 Mon–Sat

⬥ Pick out some shoes to go with that flamenco dress

La Alacena Real Old grocer's-cum-delicatessen selling fine wines, olive oils, cheeses, hams and other fine Spanish foods. Any product can be vacuum packed on the premises for safe transport home. ⓐ Pajaritos 11 ◑ 11.00–15.00, 18.00–22.00 Mon–Fri

Casa Rodriguez Statues of saints, icons and sundry religious objects. ⓐ Francos 35 ◑ 10.00–13.30, 17.00–20.30 Mon–Fri, 10.00–14.00 Sat

Compás Sur Mainly a place to buy recordings of flamenco, this shop will also set you up with flamenco guitar or dance classes. ⓐ Cuesta del Rosario 7, between Plaza del Alfalfa and Plaza de Salvador ◑ 10.30–14.30, 17.30–22.00 Mon–Sat

El Corte Inglés Spain's leading department store on eight floors with a restaurant and supermarket stocked with delicacies. ⓐ Plaza del Duque de la Victoria 8 ◐ 954 59 70 00 ◑ 10.00–22.00 Mon–Sat

Embrujo Sevillano Souvenirs of Seville: t-shirts, fans, jewellery and accessories such as scarves, embroidered shawls and castanets. ⓐ Branches at Miguel de Mañara 11b and 16, Pasaje de Vila 2, Mateos Gago 15 and Alcaicería 26 ◑ 10.00–21.00 Mon–Sat

Flamenco Cool If you're secretly thinking all those lurid colours and flouncy dresses are verging on the kitsch, this is a shop for you. Dancing shoes with wings, over-the-top candles, postmodern bullfighters' capes and spots to create your own flamenco bling. ⓐ Amor de Dios 14 ◑ 10.00–14.30, 17.30–21.00 Mon–Fri, 11.00–14.30, 18.00–21.30 Sat

Mango This chain selling fashion for the young urban woman has five shops in Seville, this one among them. ⓐ Velazquez 7–9 ⓛ 10.00–21.00 Mon–Sat

Sevillarte A ceramics and handicraft centre selling traditional and new designs. Also stocks Lladró porcelain (made in Valencia). ⓐ Sierpes 66 ⓛ 10.00–13.30, 16.30–20.15 Mon–Sat

Zara A Spanish institution because of its affordable fashion for women, men and children. ⓐ Plaza del Duque de la Victoria 1 ⓛ 10.00–20.30 Mon–Sat

TAKING A BREAK

Cafés & ice creams
Ochoa £ ❶ An old cake shop and tea room which serves homemade ice creams and claims to serve the best milkshakes in Seville. ⓐ Sierpes 45

Rayas £ ❷ Seville's most renowned ice cream shop for its homemade products. ⓐ Almirante Apodaca 1

La Campana ££ ❸ Seville's oldest café-cum-cake shop: a landmark on the square of the same name at the end of Calle Sierpes. ⓐ Sierpes 1

Bars & tapas
Casa Morales £ ❹ The city's second oldest bar, and a good place to eat tapas and taste wines. ⓐ Garcia de Vinuesa 11

Europa £ ❺   Not just a good place for tapas at any time of day but also it opens early (08.00) and serves a hearty breakfast for an all-in price. ⓐ Siete Revuelta 35, Plaza del Pan behind Salvador church close to Plaza Alfalfa

La Estrella ££ ❻   Long-standing bar famed for tapas way beyond the mundane, such as its award-winning aubergine covered with fried tomatoes, peppers, onions, chopped prawns, hard boiled egg and bechamel sauce and served au gratin. ⓐ Estrella 3, near Argote de Molina

Giralda ££ ❼   Exquisite tapas including mushroom and cod pie, stuffed courgettes, sirloin stuffed with ham, egg and parsley, and 'Seville's most famous stuffed peppers'. ⓐ Mateos Gago 1

Modesto ££ ❽   A bar and restaurant facing across a square. A couple of doors down from the bar is the Mercader de Ambar making *churros* (batter sticks) which can be eaten at one of the tables of the bar if you order a *café con leche* or hot chocolate to go with them. ⓐ Cano y Cueto 5

AFTER DARK

Restaurants
La Habanita £ ❾   Cuban food including vegan and vegetarian options. ⓐ Golfo 3, near Plaza Alfalfa ⓣ 954 21 95 16

Baco ££ ❿   Part of a mini catering empire consisting of five restaurants specialising in Andalucian cuisine, a bar, a hotel and a chain of delicatessen supermarkets. ⓐ Francos 42 ⓣ 954 21 11 31

Hostería del Laurel ££ ⓫   Supposedly the place where Zorillo was inspired to write *Don Juan Tenorio*. A good place for tapas or a full meal at outdoor tables in one of Santa Cruz's picturesque squares. Also a hotel (see page 36). ⓐ Plaza de los Venerables 5 ⓣ 954 22 02 95

La Alicantina ££ ⓬   Bar and restaurant in which the menu is especially strong on fish and seafood. Large terrace. Vegetarians catered for. ⓐ Plaza del Salvador 2 ⓣ 954 22 61 22

La Judería ££ ⓭   Highly rated restaurant for a special lunch or night out. Traditional Andalucian cuisine. Large selection of wines. ⓐ Cano y Cueto 13 ⓣ 954 42 64 56

Becerrita £££ ⓮   Sevillian cuisine and tapas. ⓐ Recaredo 9 (Puerta Carmona) ⓣ 954 41 20 57 ⓛ Closed Sun night

Casa Robles £££ ⓯   A chain of four establishments, including a tapas bar. ⓐ Alvarez Quintero 58 ⓣ 954 21 31 50

Egāna-Oriza £££ ⓰   Usually classed as Seville's most highly rated restaurant. The cuisine is a fusion of Basque and Andalucian. ⓐ San Fernando 41 ⓣ 954 22 72 11

La Albahaca £££ ⓱   Atmospheric and elegant restaurant in a beautiful old 1920s house. ⓐ Plaza Santa Cruz 12 ⓣ 954 22 07 14

Bars
Abades Night-time drinking bar in an 18th-century mansion. ⓐ Abades 13 ⓣ 954 22 56 22 ⓛ Opens 17.00

Flamenco shows

Casa de la Memoria de Al Andalus A well-respected centre for the study of Andalucian culture. 🅐 Ximenez de Enciso 28 🅣 954 56 06 70 🕒 Show starts 21.00

El Palacio Andaluz Dinner plus a flamenco show makes for an expensive night out. A cheaper alternative is just to have a drink with the show. 🅐 Avenida Maria Auxiliadora 18 🅣 954 53 47 20 🕒 Shows at 19.00 and 22.00

La Carbonería This bar in the premises of a former coal merchant is a well-known place to hear and see flamenco. 🅐 Levies 18 🅣 954 21 44 60 🕒 10.00–15.00

Los Gallos Claims to keep it simple and authentic. 🅐 Plaza de Santa Cruz 11 🅣 954 21 69 81 🕒 Shows (lasting 2 hours) at 20.00 and 22.30

Clubs

Catedral One of the few clubs in the city centre, this one plays on a religious theme. The music is mainly hip hop, house and R&B. 🅐 Cuesta del Rosario 🅣 954 22 85 90 🕒 11.00–06.00 Wed–Sun

Beyond the centre

Beyond the dense streets of the Santa Cruz quarter and around the cathedral and Reales Alcázares the sights of Seville certainly thin out but there are still many of them to see as well as shops, bars, restaurants and clubs aplenty.

To the north, Santa Cruz merges into the large workaday district of La Macarena. There are several churches here, but the only real sight is the basilica of La Macarena – home to a fervent cult of the Virgin Mary, which stands next to a surviving stretch of the city walls.

Head towards the river from Santa Cruz and the cathedral, on the other hand, and you are immediately in El Arenal, the former docksides. Here are two of the city's most distinctive monuments: the bullring and the Torre del Oro.

Follow the river and you will come to another interesting area of sightseeing: the vast area of greenery which is the Parque de María Luisa.

East from Santa Cruz, across Calle Menendez y Pelayo, the sights vanish (unless you are interested in football), but you might well be drawn to this modern part of the city by its growing number of shops, bars and nightspots.

SIGHTS & ATTRACTIONS

Basílica de La Macarena

Seville has always had a strong cult of the Virgin Mary. It has two rival statues of the mother of Jesus which are ceremoniously brought out during the Holy Week processions. One of them resides in Triana. The other, possibly more famous, is housed here in this baroque church built in 1949. The statue was carved in the late 17th

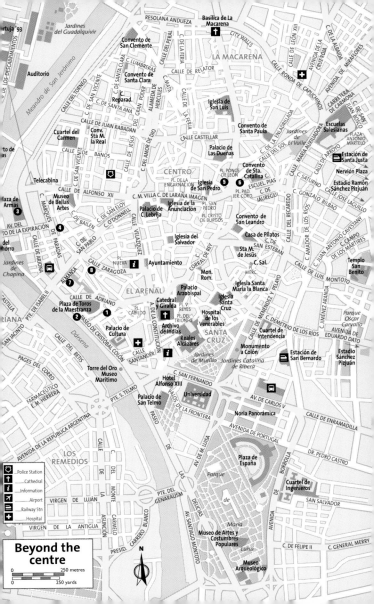

century, probably by the sculptress Luisa Roldán (or La Roldana), and its expression is said to be something between a smile and sadness. There's a museum dedicated to the Virgin de la Macarena and the Brotherhood, which maintains her cult as well as a shop selling devotional items.

The city walls next to the Basilica were built by the Almoravides (Moors) in the 11th century. Most of the towers and gates were pulled down in the 19th century leaving just this fragment.

ⓐ Calle Bécquer 1 ⓣ 954 90 18 00

ⓦ www.hermandaddelamacarena.org ⓛ 09.00–14.00 Mon–Fri, 17.00–20.00 Sat, 09.30–14.00, 17.00–21.00 Sun

Hotel Alfonso XIII

Seville's premier guesthouse is thought to be the only hotel ever commissioned by a reigning monarch, having been built on the orders of Alfonso XIII for heads of state visiting the 1929 Ibero–American exhibition. He is lucky to have been immortalised in the name of such a place, as in real life he was not so fortunate. His insensitive meddling in political and military affairs forced him to abdicate in 1931 and go into exile. The hotel is in neo-Moorish style with a central courtyard, sumptuous salons, grand corridors, an ornate lift, elegant stained glass panels, crystal chandeliers and many other exquisite decorative touches. You are welcome to stroll around (it's a good place to escape from the heat and traffic noise) or have a drink in the bar.

ⓐ San Fernando 2 ⓣ 954 91 70 00 (see page 37)

ⓞ *Seville's Plaza de Toros is the most famous bullring in the world*

Noria Panorámica (Wheel of Seville)

This 60-m (197-ft) tall big wheel came into operation in 2006 and provides the highest vantage point from which to get a sweeping view of the city. It has 42 cabins taking up to 8 people each. One of them is a VIP cabin, equipped with leather furniture, plasma screen TV and DVD, telephone and fridge containing champagne. Each revolution lasts 12 minutes, so make the most of them.

ⓐ Jardines del Prado de San Sebastián

ⓦ www.noriapanoramicadesevilla.com ⓣ 10.00–24.00

Parque de María Luisa & the Plaza de España

In 1929 the city of Seville decided to transform a swathe of the grounds of the 17th-century Palacio de San Telmo into a fairground for the Ibero–American exhibition, a grand venture that didn't quite pay off at the time because the world was heading for depression – this was the year of the Wall Street Crash – but which bequeathed the city some extraordinary architecture as well as a superb park.

In particular, the Plaza de España is Seville at its extravagant, monumental best: a large semicircle of arcades ending in two mock baroque towers borrowed from the pilgrimage city of Santiago de Compostela in northern Spain. But what makes the Plaza de España shine, literally, are its ceramics. Following the curve of the building on the lowest level are technicoloured tiled benches representing the provinces of Spain in alphabetical order. The banisters of the bridges across its canal, meanwhile, are mini-masterpieces of the ceramicist's art.

Plaza de Toros de la Maestranza

Built in 1761, Seville's bullring is one of the oldest in Spain and certainly the most famous in the world. The bullring is owned by the Real Maestranza de Caballería (the Royal Corps of the Order of Chivalry of Seville), an organisation created around the time of the Reconquest to prepare and arm mounted knights for battle. It is a curious structure, not circular as might be expected but an irregular polygon made up of 30 sides of varying lengths with a white and ochre vernacular baroque façade looking onto the river bank. A capacity crowd is 13,934 spectators.

◆ *Exuberant ceramics at the Plaza de España*

The arena itself is egg-shaped with the ground in it slightly higher in the centre than at the edges. Around the ring are all the facilities needed by the world of bullfighting: rooms for the *toreros* and their teams, a chapel (bullfighters are invariably deeply pious), infirmary, bull pens, a 'skinnery' and so on. The 20-minute guided visit takes in the highlights of the complex and the museum. This contains *trajes de luces* ('suits of lights' – the bullfighters' stunning outfits), paintings, bulls' heads and other bullfighting treasures.

The bullfighting season traditionally begins on Easter Sunday and ends in October. If you want to attend, there is a bewildering choice of seats. The cheapest are the top *gradas* in full sun (*sol*); the most expensive are those close to the ring in the shade (*sombra*). ⓐ Paseo de Cristóbal Colón ☎ 954 22 45 77 (for tickets to see a bullfight ☎ 954 50 13 82) ⓦ www.realmaestranza.com ⏱ 09.30–19.00

Torre del Oro

There's not much to this short, 12-sided tower on the banks of the River Guadalquivir north of the Puente de San Telmo, but it is still a well-known landmark of the city. It was built in the 13th century by the Almohad rulers of southern Spain as part of their defences for the city. A twin tower stood on the opposite bank and a chain slung between the two prevented enemy vessels from sailing up the river. Why exactly it is called 'the Tower of Gold' is anyone's guess. It may be because it was once clad in gold tiles. Or it may be because it witnessed so many tonnes of New World gold unloaded on the dockside beside it. At various times in its history it has served as

● *The 13th-century Torre del Oro stands on the banks of the Guadalquivir*

wharf building, lighthouse, prison, house and chapel. Currently, it is a naval museum.

🅐 Paseo de Cristóbal Colón ☏ 954 22 24 19 🕐 10.00–14.00 Tues–Fri, 11.00–14.00 Sat & Sun. Free on Tues

Universidad (Royal Tobacco Factory)

One of the most prized discoveries of the New World was tobacco; by the 18th century it was being universally chewed and smoked all over Europe. The majority of the continent's cigarettes were produced here in this vast, palatial factory building, which was completed in 1771 and now serves as part of Seville University. It can be hard to imagine the lives of the 3,000 female workers, *cigarreras*,

---

CARMEN

It's almost impossible to think of Seville's bullring without also thinking of Carmen, the tragic heroine of Bizet's opera of the same name. The story is based on an 1845 novella by Prosper Mérimée, who was inspired by a true story he heard from a countess while he was travelling in Spain. The eponymous Carmen is a strong-willed, mesmerising, manipulative young siren who attracts the attentions of a soldier, Don José, who is so besotted with her that he abandons his regiment. Carmen, however, spurns him in favour of a virile bullfighter, Escamillo. In a jealous rage, Don José springs on Carmen outside the bullring's Puerta del Principe and kills her as the crowds cheer Escamillo performing in the ring. The opera has proved to have an enduring appeal because it avoids easy moralising and Carmen, for all her faults, is likeable for her passion and her acceptance of her fate.

who spent long working days rolling cigarettes on their thighs. Indeed, we probably wouldn't give them a second thought had they not inspired the world's most enduring musical (see box).

ⓐ San Fernando ☏ 954 55 10 00 🕐 08.30–22.30 Mon–Sat. Admission free

CULTURE

Museo Arqueológico & Museo de Artes y Costumbres Populares

At the far end of the Parque de María Luisa from the city, two museums face each other across the Plaza de America, both of them occupying pavilions built for the 1929 exhibition. The more interesting is the archaeological museum, a neo-Renaissance building in which the exhibits include the Treasure of the Carambolo – a collection of jewellery from the semi-mythical civilisation of Tartessos, which existed in Andalucia in the 8th–9th centuries BC.

The other museum, the Museo de Artes y Costumbres Populares, houses a collection of folk arts and crafts.

Both museums 🕐 14.30–20.30 Tues, 09.00–20.30 Wed–Sat, 09.00–14.30 Sun. Free to EU citizens

Museo de Bellas Artes

Seville's fine arts museum is claimed to be the second most important art gallery in Spain after the Prado in Madrid. It is housed in a 17th-century convent and has two floors arranged around three cloisters, all linked by a grand staircase. The building is appropriate since many of the works originally hung in convents and churches and are on religious themes. Although the museum has some sculpture and pieces of ceramics, jewellery and furniture (with exhibits dating from the Gothic period to the present day), the focus is on Seville's homegrown school of painting.

The core of the collection is from three masters of Sevillian baroque: Zurbarán, Murillo and Valdés Leal. Other singular works include a statue of St Jerome by the Italian sculptor Pietro Torrigiano who is more famous for having broken Michelangelo's nose while they were both students, traumatising the latter for life. Torrigiano died in the Inquisition's prison in Seville in 1522.

ⓐ Plaza del Museo 9 ☎ 954 22 07 90

ⓦ www.juntadeandalucia.es/cultura/museos/MBASE

🕐 14.30–20.30 Tues, 09.00–20.30 Wed–Sat, 09.00–14.30 Sun. Free to EU citizens

🔼 The Museo de Bellas Artes houses one of Spain's most important art collections

RETAIL THERAPY

Antonio Bernal Get yourself a Spanish guitar made to order in this guitar builder's workshop across the road from Nervión Plaza. ⓐ Hernando del Pulgar 20 ⓛ 10.00–14.00, 17.00–20.30 Mon–Fri, 10.00–14.00 Sat

Nervión Plaza Shopping centre between Santa Justa station and the football stadium. To get there on foot follow the remains of the Roman aqueduct along Calle Luis Montoto. ⓐ Avenida Luis Morales and Avenida Eduardo Dato ⓛ Shops: 10.00–22.00; restaurants 10.00–03.00

Pedro Algaba A bullfighter's tailor: suits of light for rent or sale, but good ones don't come cheap. It takes a month and a team of 40 people to make a full suit. If you just want a souvenir, there are swords, capes, hats, sticks, banderillas, symbols, handkerchiefs, key rings and posters on sale. ⓐ Adriano 39 in El Arenal, next to the Maestranza bullring ⓛ 10.15–14.00, 17.15–20.30 Mon–Fri, 10.15–14.00 Sat

Plaza de Armas A shopping and entertainment centre occupying the gracious engine shed of the former Córdoba railway station. ⓐ Plaza de la Legion ⓛ 10.00–22.00 (entertainment venues stay open later)

Seville Football Club official shop If flamenco dresses, fans and shawls are not for you, you can always take home a sporting memento of Seville. ⓐ Avenida Eduardo Dato, Estadio Ramón Sánchez Pizjuán ⓛ 10.00–21.00 Mon–Sat

TAKING A BREAK

Bodeguita Antonio Romero £ ❶ The renowned selection of Andalucian specialities on the tapas menu – including a variety of *montaditos* (toasted sandwiches) – means that this place is often crowded. ⓐ Antonio Diaz 19 ❶ 954 22 39 39 ⓐ Gamazo 16 ❶ 954 21 05 85

El Torero £ ❷ This kiosk on the river bank across the road from the bullring makes a handy refuelling stop for drinks only. It has a few tables with sunshades and plays mercifully tasteful soothing music to compete with the traffic roar. ⓐ Paseo de Cristóbal Colón

La Fábrica de la Cerveza £ ❸ No queues; no waiting: in this microbrewery bar you serve the beer yourself at a tap installed at your table. To go with the homebrew you can order tapas or a full meal. ⓐ Centro Comercial Plaza de Armas ❶ 954 90 88 28

Las Piletas £ ❹ As it opens at 07.00, this is a useful place to have breakfast. Later, tapas take over. ⓐ Marques de Paradas 28 ❶ 954 22 04 04

El Rinconcillo £ ❺ Seville's oldest bar is also one of its most atmospheric. ⓐ Gerona 40 ❶ 954 22 31 83

Taberna Manzanilla £ ❻ This small bar has tables spread in the triangular square across the road from El Rinconcillo. It has a good menu of tapas and also rents out rooms if you are in need of somewhere to stay. ⓐ Plaza de Terceros 7 (Sol 17) ❶ 954 22 45 93

▶ *Great ham and great atmosphere at El Rinconcillo, Seville's oldest bar*

AFTER DARK

Restaurants

Asador Salas £ ❼ Meat, fish and shellfish grilled over a fire of smouldering holm oakwood. ⓐ Almansa 15 ❶ 954 21 77 96

Taberna del Alabardero £££ ❽ As well as a highly regarded elegant formal restaurant whose menu changes four times a year with the seasons, there is a café-bistro with a cool tiled interior where a shorter version of the same menu is served. Also a hotel (see page 39). ⓐ Zaragoza 20 ❶ 954 50 27 21

Live music

Fun Club Seville's oldest venue begins the night with a concert and continues it as a bar. Eclectic agenda from ethnic to electro.
ⓐ Alameda de Hercules 86 ❶ 650 48 98 58 ❷ 24.00–06.00 Thur/Fri, 24.00–07.00 Fri/Sat

Nuyor A converted 19th-century building in which everything – down to the cocktails, coffee and cigars – is meant to make you feel you are in colonial Cuba. Live Caribbean band each night.
ⓐ Café Marqués de Paradas 30 ❶ 954 21 28 89 ❷ 15.30–late Tues–Sun

Terraza Capote A great place to be on a spring or summer evening. On Tuesdays you can enjoy flamenco with your cocktail and on Wednesdays it's theatre. Thursdays are given over to live Latin music. ⓐ Marqués de Contadero, next to puente de Triana
❶ 954 56 38 58 ❷ 12.00 to the early hours

Flamenco shows

El Arenal Having been in business since 1950, this is one of Seville's longest running flamenco venues. ⓐ Rodo 7, between Arco del Postigo and the bullring ⓣ 954 21 64 92 ⓛ Shows at 20.30 and 22.30

Casa Carmen For those looking for flamenco variety. ⓐ Marqués de Perada ⓣ 954 21 28 89 ⓦ www.casacarmenarteflamenco.com ⓛ Different 1-hour show every day 20.30

Clubs

Aduana Two dance floors playing pop on one and house, electro and techno on the other. ⓐ Avenida Raza, on the corner with Cardenal Bueno Monreal ⓣ 954 23 61 25 ⓛ 23.00 onwards

Bauhaus Café Electro-house, tech-house and nu-lounge. ⓐ Marqués de Parada 53 ⓣ 954 22 42 10 ⓛ 16.00–04.00

Buddha del Mar Chill out, funk, house, Latin and Spanish and international pop in the former railway station that is now the Plaza de Armas shopping centre. The restaurant serves Japanese, Thai and Chinese food. ⓐ Centro comercial Plaza de Armas, Plaza de la Legion ⓣ 954 08 90 95 ⓛ 13.30–17.00, 21.00 to 01.00

Simonne One of many new bars and clubs proliferating along the appropriately named Avenida de la Innovación besides the city's conference and exhibition centre in the city's eastern suburbs. It plays a variety of music to dance to, but nothing too spaced out. Other places to try nearby are Templo, Hispano and Walhalla. ⓐ Avenida de la Innovación 3, Edif. Hercules ⓣ 954 07 59 36 ⓛ 16.00–02.00 Sun–Wed, 16.00–04.00 Thur, 16.00–05.00 Fri & Sat

The river & beyond

Across the Guadalquivir from the city centre the city continues as a built-up island between two branches of the river. Step off the Puente de Isabel II, built of iron in 1852, and you'll find yourself in Triana, renowned as one of the cradles of flamenco and the source of all the beautiful ceramics to be seen in Seville. There are few sights as such but, if nothing else, you'll get some great views over the river.

To the south, Triana merges into the Barrio de Los Remedios – nudging up to the site of the April Fair – which you will probably only stray into if you are looking for a particular shop, restaurant or club.

To the north, meanwhile, is the Isla de La Cartuja, an elongated strip of land rehabilitated for the Expo 92 world fair. Since that brief moment of glory, the Cartuja has been in search of a new vision to steer its future. Parts of the site have been 'repurposed' as an urban theme park and a technological business park, with offices and laboratories installed in some of expo's architecturally striking pavilions. But much of the Cartuja has a neglected feel with a disused cable car and Ariadne rocket now surrounded by fields of weeds – and not a shop, bar or restaurant in sight. In the middle of the Isla de la Cartuja stands an incongruous, schizophrenic monument: a monastery that was converted into a ceramics factory in the Industrial Revolution and now serves as a museum of contemporary art.

SIGHTS & ATTRACTIONS

Guadalquivir river & its bridges
The Guadalquivir river has formed the watery backbone of Seville since Roman times when merchant vessels sailed upstream to

The river & beyond

deposit one cargo and leave with another. Later, fleets rolled up laden with gold and silver from the New World. There is still a functioning port, but it is largely dedicated to servicing tourist cruise ships.

The best bank to stroll along is on the city centre side of the river, from the Torre de Oro to beyond the Plaza de Armas shopping centre. If you aren't feeling energetic, sit and enjoy the view from one of the bars and restaurants on Calle del Betis on the Triana side.

An even better way to enjoy the river is to take a short cruise with Cruceros Torre del Oro (see page 58).

The river is crossed by nine bridges, six of which were built for Expo 92. The two most interesting are the Puente del Alamillo

⬤ Take a cruise boat and see the city from the river

(designed by the artist Santiago Calatrava) and the Puente de la Barqueta (opposite Isla Magica theme park), the most visible reminder of the heady days of the Expo for most Sevillanos.

Isla Mágica

One of the few theme parks in the world in an urban area, the Magic Island is built around the lake that was at the heart of Expo 92. It is loosely divided into eight zones and has over 40 rides, games, shows and other attractions – including a freefall tower, a 16th-century merry-go-round, various big dippers, a llama rodeo, rafting rivers and a '4 dimension' virtual reality experience.
ℹ Information: 902 16 17 16; Reservations: 902 16 00 00
ⓦ www.islamagica.es ◕ Varies according to day of week and time of year

Triana

When you have drunk your fill of pretty-pretty Santa Cruz and seen enough of the grand monuments of central Seville, you might want to wander across the bridge into the more down-to-earth district of La Triana, which looks across the river at the bullring and the Torre del Oro. There are few historic sights here, but Triana has had plenty of history. To begin with it still bears its Roman name (deriving from Trajana, after the Emperor Trajan who was born in nearby Italica). Later, less appealingly, Triana was an early home to the Spanish Inquisition as recalled by the name of one of its streets, Callejón de la Inquisición. Being a working-class, waterside neighbourhood, Triana has always been a rich recruiting ground for sailors and adventurers and supplied many shiphands bound for the Americas.

There are three good reasons for coming to modern Triana. First, even if you get no further than the end of the bridge, you will enjoy

good views looking back at the city centre. Better still, take a seat at an outdoor table of one of the bars and restaurants along Calle del Betis, from which you can gaze at the Torre de Oro and the bullring and watch cruise ships come and go.

Second, this is the place to buy ceramics. It is the source of all the murals to be seen around central Seville and there are still around 40 functioning shops, studios, factories and workshops, most of which are open to visitors. The oldest and most popular is Cerámica Santa Ana (see page 100).

The third lure is flamenco. This is Seville's traditional gypsy quarter and proudly claims to be one of the birthplaces of flamenco

TRIANA CERAMICS

The first record of ceramics being produced in Triana dates from 1314, but it is widely accepted that the industry is much older than that. It is probable that the Romans produced amphorae here to transport oil and wine. In the Moorish period, Triana's potteries outside the city walls were busy producing the blue, white and green ceramic tiles, *azulejos*, that form such an essential part of interior decorations of buildings of the time. The characteristics of modern Triana pottery are considered to have been established by an Italian craftsman, Francisco Nicoloso Pisano, who settled in Triana at the end of the 15th century. In the 18th century, there was a great demand for painted tiles depicting religious images and realistic themes. Contemporary Triana ceramicists still make large mosaic scenes and signs for a variety of uses around the city.

◀ *Triana is the place to seek out authentic flamenco*

⬤ *The colourful façade of Cerámica Santa Ana (see page 100)*

(an honour tacitly shared with Jerez de la Frontera). Although you can see highly organised, professional shows in Santa Cruz, a purist would argue that you need to stumble on an impromptu combination of singer, guitarist and dancer swept up in the frenzy of spontaneous emotion in some uncelebrated Triana dive to understand what flamenco is really about.

CULTURE

Monasterio de Santa María de las Cuevas (Centro Andaluz de Arte Contemporaneo)

In 1248, according to tradition, a statue of the Virgin Mary was found in one of the caves north of Triana from which clay to feed the potteries was extracted. A monastery dedicated to 'Our Lady of the

Caves' grew up on the site. Columbus stayed in it, and his family had close links with it after his death. A magnificent ombu tree in its grounds is said to have been planted by Hernando Columbus, the son of the explorer.

The monastery was abandoned in 1835. Soon after the buildings were leased by Charles Pickman, a merchant from Liverpool, who built kilns and installed machinery to churn out ceramics to meet local demand. Production continued into the 1970s.

In 1992 the monastery-factory formed a centrepiece for the Expo. Since then it has housed Andalucia's contemporary art gallery, but this institution is rather cowed by its setting. At the heart of the complex is a rather plain church with a pretty Mudejar patio off it in which the pallid statues of two nuns kneel at prayer.

ELCANO'S ROUND-THE-WORLD VOYAGE

It's usually Magellan who is credited in the record books with the first circumnavigation of the globe, but this isn't quite accurate. Although he set off from Seville in command of a mission to sail around the world, he didn't make it back to claim the honour. Tragically, he was killed in a battle in the Philippines. So it was left to one his crewmen, a Spanish Basque, Juan Sebastián Elcano (whom Magellan had previously chained up and condemned to death for mutiny) to lead the expedition back to its starting point. On 8 September 1522 Elcano, along with the remaining 19 sailors from the 200 who had set out three years before, sailed into Seville on the only surviving ship of the expedition, the *Victoria*. Magellan may get all the mentions in history books, but at least Elcano has a street named after him in Triana.

But it's more the factory features that impress. A line of iron-girdered chimneys physically overshadow the other buildings, and there are various reminders that functional art was once churned out here to earn workers and masters a living. One entrance porch is entirely covered with neat rows of ornamental tiles like a salesman's samples book left permanently open. And the entrance on the river side of the monastery (not the main entrance) is a rather cute tiled gateway.

ⓐ Avenida Amérigo Vespucio 2 ⓣ 955 03 70 70 ⓦ www.caac.es
Gallery free on Tues; grounds free

RETAIL THERAPY

Cerámica Santa Ana Triana's most famous ceramics factory, which has been going since 1870. Reproduction historical pieces are available. ⓐ San Jorge 31 ⓛ 09.30–13.30, 17.00–20.30 Mon–Fri, 10.00–14.00 Sat

Tierra Nuestra Seville's first specialist wine shop and still arguably the best. ⓐ Constancia 41 ⓛ 10.00–14.00, 18.00–21.00 Mon–Sat

TAKING A BREAK

El Faro de Triana £ ❶ The Triana Lighthouse ought to be classed as one of the city's landmarks, being a yellow tower with clock turret stuck to the end of Puente de Isabel II. Squeeze through the small bar and up the stairs where there are two small terraces with tables offering unbeatable views over the river. ⓐ Puente de Isabel II ⓣ 954 33 61 92

Sol y Sombra £ ❷   One of the authentic old bars of Andalucia decorated with bullfighting posters and serving tapas such as prawns with ham and spicy sausages. ⓐ Castilla 151 ❶ 954 33 39 35

AFTER DARK

Restaurants
San Marco ££ ❸   Exquisite cuisine – Spanish with some Italian influence – in an elegant 18th-century house on the side of Calle del Betis away from the riverbank. ⓐ Betis 68 ❶ 954 28 03 10

🔺 *Al fresco dining with great views at El Faro de Triana*

Rio Grande £££ ❹   Three restaurants share terraces with more or less the same view. This one, strong on fish and seafood, is immediately next to Puente San Telmo. Next to it is the Asador de Triana and a little further on the Kiosco de las Flores. ⓐ Betis
ⓣ 954 27 39 56

Flamenco shows

Given its role in the history of flamenco, you would have thought Triana would be the best place to see the art form at its purest. And in one way that's true. The problem is tracking down authentic flamenco. All the most organised and well advertised venues are back across the river in Santa Cruz and El Arenal. In Triana you have to keep your ears open and hope you stumble upon some bar where an impromptu performer has just acquired *el duende* – the indefinable spirit or passion that can't be bought or learned. Good bars to start your search for flamenco are:

Casa Anselma ⓐ Pagés del Corro 49
El Ancla ⓐ Pagés del Corro 43
El Rejoneo ⓐ Betis 31B
La Madrugá ⓐ Calle de Salado
Lo Nuestro ⓐ Betis 31A

Clubs

Discoteca Boss A discotheque on the banks of the Guadalquivir with a variety of levels and spaces at your disposal. ⓐ Betis 67
ⓣ 954 99 01 04 ⓛ 23.00–07.00 Wed–Sat

❍ *The lovely Andalucian 'white town' of Olvera*

OUT OF TOWN
trips

Days out from Seville

There are several places easily reached by motorway, main road and, in some cases, train from Seville. Closest of them are the Roman ruins of Itálica. Another rewarding short day trip is to the equally historic but living town of Carmona. For fresh air and wildlife, meanwhile, you need to head straight for the outstanding Doñana National Park. An hour by rail or motorway south takes you into the province of Cádiz and to the city of Jerez de la Frontera, famous for its sherries, dancing horses and its flamenco music.

SIGHTS & ATTRACTIONS

Itálica

Although Seville was founded by the Romans, it is long predated by its now insignificant neighbour, Itálica, at Santiponce just beyond the northern outskirts. This municipality was founded by Scipio Africanus in 206 BC to settle veteran soldiers of the Second Punic War. It was later the birthplace of the Emperor Trajan (born in AD 53), who ruled over the empire when it was at its maximum extent.

However, Itálica still hadn't reached the peak of its importance, which came in the 2nd century AD. Then, like the rest of the Roman Empire, it fell to the barbarian invasions of the 5th century. It was further ravaged in the 8th century by the Moors and its ruins subsequently plundered for building materials, which were incorporated into the fabric of Seville. Its ruined streets and monuments are still impressive as ruins go – especially a round mosaic floor and the elliptical amphitheatre in which 25,000 spectators could cram to watch gladiatorial contests. The most

Days out from Seville

interesting finds, though, are now in museums in Seville (and some of them in Madrid).

ⓘ 955 99 73 76 **Ⓦ** www.ayto-santiponce.es **🕒** 09.00–20.00 Tues–Sat, 10.00–16.00 Sun

Carmona

The historic town of Carmona, sitting on an outcrop of rock looking over plains, is an easy day trip or even half day up the motorway from Seville. Both the Romans and their Moors have left an indelible mark on it.

From the Moorish arch of the Puerta de Sevilla (home of the tourist information office) – which lets you through what's left of the ramparts – narrow streets climb up to the main square, the Plaza San Fernando, which is lined with some fine 17th- and 18th-century houses. The upper storeys of one corner house are photogenically faced in blue tiles.

Continue in the same direction and you'll come to the Gothic Iglesia de Santa María (on Plaza del Marqués de las Torres), which retains the ablutionary patio of the former mosque and also has a Visigothic calendar. Next to it is the Museo de la Ciudad telling the story of Carmona from the Stone Age to the present day.

Further on, the town comes to an abrupt halt at another gateway, the Puerta de Córdoba, with its two octagonal towers. Beyond, the land drops steeply away. Retrace your steps and follow the signs to the *parador*, one of the state-run chain of hotels that often occupy historic buildings. This one is in the former fortress-palace of King Pedro I, which overhangs the cliff giving an unbroken view of the vast plain of sunflowers and cereals

---

◗ *The Moorish Puerta de Sevilla at Carmona*

below where, in 206 BC, Scipio defeated Hasrubal the Carthaginian in battle.

Outside the old town are two more Roman sites of interest: an amphitheatre (closed to the public, but you can see it from outside) and the Roman necropolis (🕓 08.30–14.00 Tues–Fri, 10.00–14.00 Sat, summer; 08.30–17.00 Tues–Fri, 10.00–14.00 Sat, winter; free to EU citizens). Around 250 of the 800 family tombs that lie on the hillside in between the cypress trees have been excavated and put on display. The largest have vestibules and one, the Servilia Tomb, is as big as a small villa. The so-called Elephant Tomb, meanwhile, has benches for funeral banquets and what's thought to have been a kitchen.

Tourist Information ⓐ Arco de la Puerta de Sevilla ⓣ 954 19 09 55 ⓦ www.turismo.carmona.org

Museo de la Ciudad ⓐ Palacio Marqués de las Torres, San Ildefonso ⓣ 954 14 01 88 ⓦ www.museociudad.carmona.org 🕓 11.00–14.00 Mon, 11.00–19.00 Tues–Sun. Free on Tues

Necropolis Romana ⓐ Avenida Jorge Bónsor 95 ⓣ 954 14 08 11 🕓 09.00–17.00 Tues–Fri, 10.00–14.00 Sat & Sun. Free to EU citizens

Doñana National Park

The marshes, woods and sand dunes at the mouth of the Guadalquivir river make up one of Europe's largest and most important national parks.

Access is strictly controlled to protect the wildlife (most spectacularly the lynx and imperial eagle) that clings on in this fragile habitat, but Doñana's policy is one of controlling tourism rather than excluding it altogether.

There are five visitors' centres on the fringes of the park, the one at **Aznalcázar** being the closest to Seville. Probably the best one to head for, though, is **Acebuche**, which can be reached via **El Rocío** (a town that is dead most of the year but springs to life for a big Whitsuntide pilgrimage – see page 10).

All the visitors' centres give out information and have displays about the flora and fauna in the park. But the only way to appreciate Doñana properly is to take a guided tour in a camouflaged 4 x 4 bus. The trip takes 4 hours and covers 70 km (43 miles), taking in a representative sample of all the major ecosystems of the park. An alternative way to see a little of Doñana is to take a boat trip from the Fabrica de Hielo visitors' centre at Bajo de Guía just outside Sanlúcar de Barrameda.

Of course, the wildlife you see depends on the time of year, the weather and luck. Most of the mammals in the park are difficult to spot and inevitably a lot of the interest is in the bird life. Doñana's marshes are on one of the main migration routes, and autumn and spring can be good times for birdwatching.

Aznalcázar Visitors' Centre ⏰ 10.30–19.00 summer; 10.30–18.00 winter

Acebuche Visitors' Centre ⏰ 08.00–21.00 summer; 08.00–19.00 winter

Guided tours Booking is essential. ⓐ Trips leave from Acebuche visitors' centre, which is on the road from El Rocío towards the coast ☎ 959 43 04 32 ⏰ Depart 08.30 & 17.00 Mon–Sat, June–mid-Sept; 8.30 & 15.00 Tues–Sun, mid-Sept–May

Boat trips Reservation is essential. ⓐ Depart from Bajo de Guía, Sanlúcar de Barrameda ☎ 956 36 38 13 ⓦ www.visitasdonana.com ⏰ 10.00 Nov–Feb; 10.00 & 16.00 Mar–May & Oct; 10.00 & 17.00 June–Sept

Jerez de la Frontera

It may not sound like it, but this city gave its name to the world's most popular aperitif, sherry. In fact, bodegas producing fortified wines make up one half of Jerez's tourist appeal, and dancing horses make up the rest.

The Fundación Real Escuela Andaluza de Arte Ecuestre (Royal Horse School) has got tourist management down to a fine art and if you like horses you shouldn't come away disappointed. You can take the full tour, which includes watching training sessions and visiting the stables, the tack room, the saddlery, the palace rooms, the Museum of

⬤ *Take a tour of the Bodega González Byass at Jerez*

Equestrian Arts and the Carriage Museum. Alternatively, if you are short of time or interest, you can opt for the slightly cheaper 'half visit'.

Better, though, is to see a show of the school's highly trained white steeds performing ballet routines. Best of all is to be here in May for Jerez's Feria del Caballo (Horse Fair) with its parades and dancing by both humans and animals. The soundtrack to this and other fiestas is flamenco music, of which Jerez claims to be one of the authentic cradles (along with Seville).

As for sherry, you could fill a couple of days finding out about and tasting the stuff, but if you are just curious, visit one of the big bodegas such as González Byass (home of Tío Pepe, supposedly Spain's best-known brand abroad) or Domecq.

Tourist information ⓐ Alameda Cristina, next to Claustros de Santo Domingo ⓣ 956 32 47 47 ⓦ www.webjerez.com

Fundación Real Escuela Andaluza de Arte Ecuestre ⓐ Avenida Duque de Abrantes ⓣ 956 31 80 08 ⓦ www.realescuela.org. Visits: 11.00–14.00 Mon, Wed & Fri (except in Aug); Shows: 12.00 Tues & Thu (& Fri in Aug)

Bodegas Domecq ⓐ San Ildefonso 3 ⓣ 956 15 15 00 ⓛ 10.00, 11.00, 12.00 & 13.00 Mon–Fri, 12.00 & 14.00 Sat

Bodegas Tío Pepe – González Byass ⓐ Manuel María González 12 ⓣ 956 35 70 00 ⓛ Guided tours in English: 11.30, 12.30, 13.30, 14.00, 15.30, 16.30 & 17.30; tours in Spanish (with partial explanations in English) on the hour. Admission charge including wine tasting

RETAIL THERAPY

Carmona
Beith-El A classy souvenir shop selling objects inspired by the various civilisations to settle Carmona. ⓐ Plaza de Abastos 14–15

Jerez
La Casa del Jerez Sells souvenirs of Jerez and gives you the opportunity to taste wines before you buy. ❸ Near the Real Escuela Andaluza del Arte Ecuestre Urbanizacion Divina Pastora

TAKING A BREAK

Restaurants: Carmona
Sierra Mayor £–££ This atmospheric bar restaurant specialising in cured hams occupies the old stables of the same historic mansion which contains Carmona's museum. Even if you are not female, ask for the key to the ladies' toilet to see an ingenious bit of antique plumbing. ❸ San Ildefonso 1 Palacio Marqués de las Torres (Museo de la Ciudad) ❶ 954 14 44 04

La Yedra ££ A restaurant in a pleasing courtyard near the *parador*. ❸ General Freire 8 ❶ 954 14 45 25

Restaurants: Jerez
El Gallo Azul £ A semicircular bar with dining room above commanding a view of the street life of Jerez, such as it is (it vanishes when the shops close). Domecq wines served along with hot, tasty, varied tapas. ❸ Larga 2 ❶ 956 32 61 48

La Moderna £ A fairly rudimentary bar where the wines may not be chilled and the tapas not that exciting, but where there is almost always an easy-going atmosphere mixing all age groups. There is more space at the back where an exposed section of the city wall can be seen. ❸ Larga ❶ 956 33 99 56

Juanito ££ An old bar famous for serving the best tapas in town.
ⓐ Pescadería Vieja 8 ⓣ 956 33 48 38

Restaurants: Sanlúcar de Barrameda
Mirador de Doñana ££ One of a number of waterside restaurants
with a view across the beach and river to the national park. Fish and
seafood on the menu. ⓐ Bajo de Guia, Sanlúcar de Barrameda
ⓣ 956 36 42 05

AFTER DARK

Flamenco shows: Jerez de la Frontera
La Taberna Flamenca A restaurant housed in a former bodega.
Usefully for anyone who doesn't like late nights, the show is at 14.30
most days (check times when you reserve), while you digest your
lunch. It lasts about 50 minutes. ⓐ Angostillo de Santiago 3, in front
of Iglesia de Santiago ⓣ 956 32 36 93

ACCOMMODATION

Carmona
El Rincon de las Descalzas ££–£££ A small, homely hotel around
three flowery patios in which the peace is only disturbed by the
sound of classical music and a trickling fountain. ⓐ Descalzas 1
ⓣ 954 19 11 72 ⓦ www.elrincondelasdescalzas.com

Casa de Carmona £££ A luxurious hotel that unashamedly offers a
taste of 'the lifestyle of the authentic Spanish nobility'. ⓐ Plaza de
Lasso 1 ⓣ 954 19 10 00 ⓦ www.casadecarmona.com

Parador £££ The principal monument of Carmona, its 14th-century castle, is also its finest hotel with a tremendous view over the plains. At the foot of the cliff is the *parador's* enticing swimming pool. ⓐ Alcázar del Rey Don Pedro ① 954 14 10 10 ⓦ www.parador.es

Jerez de la Frontera
Palacio Garvey ££–£££ Restored 1850 neoclassical mansion in the old part of Jerez. Small swimming pool. No time limit for breakfast. Access for disabled guests. ⓐ Plaza Rafael Rivero, Tornería 24 ① 956 32 67 00 ⓦ www.sferahoteles.net

Bellas Artes £££ An old stone house restored using authentic materials. Individually styled rooms. Private car park for guests. ⓐ Plaza del Arroyo 45 ① 956 34 84 30 ⓦ www.hotelbellasartes.com

El Rocío
El Cortijo de los Mimbrales £££ A relaxing country estate hotel, ideal for use as a base for exploring the Doñana National Park. Exquisite 'Arabic' swimming pool surrounded by lawns, shady patios, gardens and restaurant. Various activities available. ⓐ Carretera El Rocío – Matalascañas (A-483), 3 km (2 miles) from El Rocío ① 959 44 22 37 ⓦ www.cortijomimbrales.com

Sanlúcar de Barrameda
Los Helechos ££ A friendly, bright, white, plant-filled hotel in the town from which the Doñana boat excursions depart. ⓐ Madre de Dios 9 ① 956 36 76 55 ⓦ www.hotelhelechos.com

● *Jerez cathedral from a shady side street*

The white towns

Brilliantly whitewashed hill towns and villages, often occupying dramatic sites and invariably laid out higgledy-piggledy across the contours, are emblematic of Andalucia. The most picturesque of *los pueblos blancos* are concentrated in the sierras of Cádiz province, southeast of Seville, within the range of an overnight trip from the city.

Most of these towns are imbued with the atmosphere of the Muslim inhabitants who laid out them out, and several are still looked down upon by indomitable medieval fortresses. Their narrow, shady streets have changed little over the centuries, the windows of the houses protected by wrought iron grilles which are hung with pots of geraniums.

You can get to the largest towns by public transport, but you'll need a car to explore properly. For a swift tour of the prettiest white towns take the motorway towards Jerez de la Frontera. From there turn onto the main road to Arcos de la Frontera. Here a side road branches off for El Bosque and Grazalema. A scenic road climbs over the pass between Grazalema to Zahara de la Sierra. From there you can pick up the main road again for Ronda, perhaps making a detour to see the a typical Setenil de las Bodegas.

As these towns and villages, with their tapering alleys, steps and dead ends at every turn, were built long before cars were ever thought of, it's best to park outside and walk in.

And if the towns themselves were not reason enough for a tour, the intervening countryside is often ruggedly spectacular. Once it was prowled by bandits and smugglers who took advantage of the forbidding contours. Now the mountains make excellent territory for hiking, biking and nature-watching. This corner of Spain is strikingly green and wooded, and the air smells clean. Much of this

route is within the Parque Natural Sierra de Grazalema nature reserve.

Information Office for the Parque Natural Sierra de Grazalema
ⓐ Avenida de la Diputación, El Bosque ⓣ 956 71 60 63

◓ *The old town at Arcos de la Frontera*

SIGHTS & ATTRACTIONS

Arcos de la Frontera

The point of access to the white towns from Seville is Arcos de la Frontera, which, despite the expanding modern estates of houses around its fringes, has an unchanging old heart at the top of the town where the buildings creep right up to the lip of a breathtaking precipice.

Park in the Plaza de España if you are travelling by car and walk up Calle Corredera to the main square of the old part of town, the Plaza del Cabildo. This is overlooked by the church of Santa Maria de la Asuncion, whose Platuresque west façade takes on a golden glow in the afternoon sun. To one side of the square a balcony provides views over the countryside below. Most of Arcos' shops, bars, hotels and restaurants are in the narrow streets around the Plaza del Cabildo.

Tourist Information ⓐ Plaza del Cabildo ⓣ 956 70 22 64
ⓦ www.ayuntamientoarcos.org

Cueva de la Pileta

This extensive cave contains some of the best and most curious prehistoric art in Europe: symbols in yellow and red; 360 feathery characters that may be some kind of writing (although the language may never be deciphered); and representations of animals, including a large fish.

The paintings here were created at the same time as, or perhaps even earlier than, the more famous ones at Altamira in northern Spain. However, their significance, as with all prehistoric art, remains a matter of conjecture.

Visits are by guided tour only, lasting around 1 hour. Numbers are limited, but it is possible to reserve a place by phone only on the

first tour of the day; at other times, check in advance for the tour times, then get there as early as possible.

a 4.5 km (3 miles) from Benajoan off the MA501 towards Cortes de la Frontera **t** 952 16 73 43 **w** www.cuevadelapileta.org

Grazalema

It may well be raining when you visit Grazalema because this is the place with the highest rainfall in Spain (by quantity of water falling, not number of wet days). That said, at least it keeps the surrounding countryside green.

Overlooked by crags of limestone, the town is used as a base by visitors to the nearby nature reserve of the same name, which is good for birdwatching, botanising or just walking around. The town itself has a small traditional weaving industry making blankets (see page 124).

From Grazalema, a scenic road climbs over Las Palomas Pass (1,357 m/4,452 ft) giving stunning views. On the way up you go through forests that harbour a rare species of tree, the Spanish fir (*Abies pinsapo*). It grows only in four locations over 1,000 m (3,281 ft) and they are kept under guard. Above the cliffs you are likely to see vultures soaring overhead.

Tourist information **a** Plaza de España 11 **t** 956 13 22 25

Ronda

It's hard to imagine a more dramatic site for a town than on the edge of a cliff and astride a gorge. Ronda is justly the most famous of the white towns and also the most touristy because of its proximity to the Costa del Sol.

The town is literally cut in two by a 90-m (295-ft) deep gorge (El Tajo) of the River Guadalevín. Puente Nuevo (New Bridge), a feat

◔ *A cortijo, or farmhouse, near Arcos*

of 18th-century engineering, crosses it. Its central section was once used as a prison. To get the best view of it, take the path down into the gorge from Plaza del Campillo (at the end of Calle Tenorio) or drive down Camino de los Molinos (from the Almocabar Gate) and climb up to the Arabic Arch. A visitors' centre explains the history of the bridge with an audiovisual presentation.

The next most popular sight in Ronda is the Plaza de Toros (bullring), which is the oldest in Spain and contains a bullfighting museum. The standard, modern form of bullfighting – on foot rather than on horseback – originated in Ronda in the 18th century, and this is commemorated by a 'Goya-esque' bullfight in period dress in

September. Ronda has produced two famous 'dynasties' of bullfighters, the Romeros and the Ordóñezs. Arguably the most successful bullfighter ever was Pedro Romero, who retired in 1799

🔵 *The incredible el Tajo gorge at Ronda*

remarking: 'Bearing in mind the 28 years that I have been killing bulls, on average 200 bulls a year, I reckon that I have killed approximately 5,600 bulls, if not more.' And all without suffering a single scratch. Attached to the bullring is a museum of bullfighting, the Museo Taurino.

The town has half a dozen other museums, of which the two most interesting are the Museo Lara (a private collection of antiques displayed in an aristocratic palace) and the Museo del Bandolero (whose theme is banditry in the surrounding mountains).

One other essential sight is the best-preserved suite of Moorish baths (Baños Árabes) in Spain, which have brick horseshoe arches holding up barrel vaults pierced with star-shaped skylights.

Tourist Information ⓐ Paseo de Blas Infante ☏ 952 18 71 19
ⓦ www.turismoderonda.es

Baños Árabes ⓐ Barrio de Padre Jesús, below Puente Viejo ☏ 656 95 09 37 ⓛ 10.00–19.00 Mon–Fri, 10.00–15.00 Sat & Sun. Free on Sun

Plaza de Toros y Museo Taurino ⓐ Plaza Teniente Arce ☏ 952 87 41 32 ⓛ 10.00–20.00

Museo Lara ⓐ Armiñán 29 ☏ 952 87 12 63 ⓛ 10.30–20.00

Museo del Bandolero ⓐ Calle Armiñán 65 ☏ 952 87 77 85 ⓛ 10.30–20.00

Setenil de las Bodegas

Setenil is an atypical white town because of its site. Rather than being high up on a crag or hillside it winds through a gorge, using the rock overhangs as roofs for some of its houses and transforming one street into a tunnel. In the middle of it is a 16th-century church on a rock next to an Arab tower, from the battlements of which you can get a view of the town.

Tourist information ⓐ Villa 2 ☏ 956 13 42 61

Zahara de la Sierra

A compact zig-zag cluster of white houses at the base of a rock crowned by a castle, Zahara has a strong claim to be the prettiest of the white towns. There are not many streets, but they are pleasant to stroll around. Naturally, there are great views from the castle if you can face a stiff 10–15-minute walk. At Corpus Christi (May or June) the streets of Zahara are decorated with an impressive mass of greenery brought in from the surrounding countryside.

RETAIL THERAPY

Artesanía Textil de Grazalema Maintains the traditional woollen industry. Its small factory, in which blankets and ponchos are woven from local wool using hand-operated looms, is open to the public. Products are on sale in a shop on the premises. ❷ Carretera de Ronda, Grazalema ● 08.00–14.00, 15.00–18.30 Mon–Thur, morning only on Fri; closed in Aug

TAKING A BREAK

Bars: Ronda
El Portón Popular bar for its home cooking, the speciality being bull's tail. ❷ Pedro Romero 7 ❶ 952 87 74 20 ● Closed Sun

La Giralda A Ronda institution for its varied tapas. ❷ Calle Nueva 19 ❶ 952 87 28 02 ● Closed Wed

Restaurants: Arcos de la Frontera
El Convento £ A restaurant in a 17th-century palace with a small hotel in an adjacent building. ❷ Marqués de Torresoto 7 ❶ 956 70 32 22

Mesón el Patio £ An efficient family-run restaurant in the old part of town serving traditional homemade food. There's a choice of four set menus all at the same very reasonable price. There's also a *pensión* in which some of the rooms have terraces with views.
ⓐ Callejón de las Monjas 4 ⓣ 956 70 23 02

Restaurants: Ronda
Flores £ Dependable, inexpensive place to eat. ⓐ Virgen de la Paz 9
ⓣ 952 87 10 40

Tragabuches £££ Named after a legendary bandit, this is Ronda's most highly regarded restaurant at a commensurate price.
ⓐ Calle Jose Aparicio 1 ⓣ 952 12 02 91 ⓛ Closed Sun night and Mon

Restaurants: Setenil de las Bodegas
Las Flores £ A village bar-restaurant serving straightforward but wholesome food. ⓐ Avenida del Carmen ⓣ 956 12 40 44

ACCOMMODATION

Arcos de la Frontera
La Casa Grande £–££ Boutique hotel in the old part of town with a rooftop terrace for relaxing. ⓐ Maldonaldo 10 ⓣ 956 70 39 30
ⓦ www.lacasagrande.net

Marqués de Torresoto £–££ A comfortable 17th-century aristocratic house in the old part of town next to the church and the main square. Restaurant in the patio. ⓐ Marques de Torresoto 4
ⓣ 956 70 07 17 ⓦ www.hmdetorresoto.com

Grazalema

La Casa de las Piedras £ A converted house in one of the oldest streets in the town. The bedrooms, around a patio, are simply but charmingly furnished and the beds spread with locally made Grazalema blankets. Lounge with fireplace. Six modern apartments further down the street are available for rent. There is a restaurant, but this is under separate management. ⓐ Calle de las Piedras 32 ⓣ 956 13 20 14 ⓦ www.casadelaspiedras.net

⬥ *Horses graze in an olive grove near Ronda*

Ronda

Arriadh £–££ A five-room hotel with views near Arriate, just outside Ronda. ⓐ Camino de Laura ⓣ 952 11 43 70
ⓦ www.andalucia.com/arriadh

Alavera de los Banos ££ Homely small hotel next to the Arab baths. Swimming pool. Some rooms have a private terrace. ⓐ San Miguel
ⓣ 952 87 91 43 ⓦ www.andalucia.com/alavera

Molino del Santo ££–£££ Once a watermill, now a peaceful sun-trap with a pleasing swimming pool. ⓐ Benaojan ⓣ 952 16 71 51
ⓦ www.molinodelsanto.com

Molino del Arco £££ Family-run guesthouse in a converted olive oil mill. ⓐ Partido de los Frontones, 8 km (5 miles) from Ronda
ⓣ 952 11 40 17 ⓦ www.hotelmolinodelarco.com

Reina Victoria £££ Historically, the grand hotel of Ronda – and still retaining some of its turn-of-the-century elegance and charm. The extensive garden and terrace give great views over the surrounding countryside. ⓐ Jerez 25 ⓣ 952 87 12 40

Zahara de la Sierra

Marqués de Zahara £ Large old house around a central patio converted into an 11-room hotel and restaurant. ⓐ San Juan 3
ⓣ 956 12 30 61 ⓦ www.marquesdezahara.com

Córdoba & Granada

Seville is one of the three great cities of Andalucia associated with the medieval Muslim civilisation of Spain. It would be a shame to go away without seeing the other two, Córdoba and Granada. They are easily reached by motorway and have one world-famous monument apiece plus a host of other sights worth visiting. Don't worry about overdosing on cultural sightseeing: all three cities are very different in atmosphere and accordingly they complement each other perfectly. They are also packed with bars and restaurants.

An overnight stay is advisable for each of the two away cities, although you could do Córdoba in a day and get back to Seville for the night. Best of all is to link everything up in a triangular three-day tour with optional stopovers. Before setting out for Granada, be sure to reserve your visit to the Alhambra.

SIGHTS & ATTRACTIONS

Antequera

This ancient town at the crossroads between Seville, Granada, Malaga and Córdoba has two clusters of monuments. One is uphill from the tourist information office through a formal 16th-century gateway, the Arco de los Gigantes (Giants' Arch), and includes the Renaissance church of Real Colegiata de Santa María la Mayor and the remains of a Muslim fortress, the Alcazaba.

Far older than anything else you will see in Andalucia are three impressive dolmens on the edge of town. The largest is the Dolmen de Menga dating from 2500 BC. However, the most interesting is the Dolmen de Romeral because of its domed chamber – the first case of intentional architectural construction in Europe.

Tourist information ⓐ Plaza San Sebastián ⓣ 952 70 81 42
ⓦ www.antequera.es
Dolmens ⓐ On the road out towards Archidona ⓛ 09.00–18.00
Tues–Sat, 09.30–14.30 Mon

Córdoba

Roman Córdoba was the capital of southern Spain and the
birthplace of the poet Lucan and the philosopher Seneca. But it was
after the Muslim invasion of Spain in the 8th century that it truly
came into its own. In 929 Abd al-Rahman III declared himself caliph
of Spain, with Córdoba as his capital. In the 10th and 11th centuries,
while the rest of Europe was wallowing in the dark ages, the
civilised place to be was in Muslim Córdoba where Christians and
Jews added to a cultural melting pot, and art and learning thrived.

The magnificence that once was can be seen in the famous
mezquita (mosque) that dominates the city centre and is one of
the key sights of Andalucia. The mosque was built on the site of a
Visigothic church and is the work of four caliphs. What impresses is
the immense size of the Hall of Caliph Abd al-Rahman. It is the only
building on the site that has a roof, which is supported by over 800
two-tier horseshoe arches rising from slender columns (many of
which are recycled from Roman and Visigothic buildings). Because
the whole area slopes downhill, you enter from above, and the Hall
is near the bottom. On the southern wall is a *mihrab* – prayer niche
decorated with intricate plasterwork and mosaics.

When Córdoba was reconquered by the Christians they couldn't
leave such a structure untouched to testify to the success of their
rival religion. Thus, in the 16th century a cathedral was dropped
incongruously into the middle of the Hall. The old minaret was
simultaneously dressed up as a belfry.

For a more down to earth appreciation of medieval Córdoba, take a walk around the Judería, the old Jewish quarter of the city near the mosque. This is a delightful jumble of shady alleyways and whitewashed houses decorated with wrought iron grilles and flowerpots. Look out for the *Sinagoga* (synagogue), no more than a delightful square hall with richly decorated walls, and one of the only three remaining in Spain. Many of them have secretive patios that are opened to the public in a special fiesta in May.

There is just one drawback to visiting Córdoba: parking. If you are visiting for the day by car, the best policy is to head for the underground multi-storey car park (ⓐ Avenida del Aeropuerto – which, as its name says, goes towards the airport), 15 minutes' walk from the monuments.

Tourist information ⓐ Caballerizas Reales 1 ⓣ 957 20 17 74 ⓦ www.turismodecordoba.org

Mezquita ⓐ Cardenal Herrero 1 ⓣ 957 47 05 12 ⓛ Best to check these in advance, as they can change. Free 08.30–10.00 on weekdays

Sinagoga ⓣ 957 20 29 28 ⓛ 09.30–14.00, 15.30–17.30 Tues–Sun. Free to EU citizens

Écija

Écija makes a useful stopover on the way to or from Córdoba, as it is just off the N4 motorway. In particular, it has 11 churches with baroque steeples. All the main sights can be reached on foot from the main square, the Plaza de España.

Tourist information ⓐ Palacio de Benamejí

Museo Histórico Municipal ⓐ Cánovas del Castillo 4 ⓣ 955 90 29 33 ⓦ www.ecija.es

Granada

As the last Muslim city of Spain to fall to the Christian Reconquest (in 1492), Granada had time to see its civilisation mature before being eclipsed. The result is the Alhambra, an exquisite palace-fortress that sits on a hill above the city. You can get a good view of it from the atmospheric Albaicin quarter, a cluster of narrow streets and handsome houses.

There is plenty more to see in Granada, but if you have only a day, it's best to spend most of it exploring the Alhambra. Allow at least three hours for a visit. The complex is made up of three parts: the fortress or Alcazaba, the summer palace of the Generalife (of interest mainly for its gardens) and the Royal or Nazrid Palace. This last part, an exquisite assembly of patios and intricately decorated halls mostly built in the 14th century, is what everyone comes to see. Visitor numbers are restricted and it is essential to book ahead.

In the hubbub of the city centre is the exquisite royal funerary chapel, the Capilla Real. Equally attractive in its own way is the half-hidden Corral del Carbón, a 14th-century Moorish *caravanserai* later used as a coal store, from which it gets its present name.

Tourist information ⓐ Santa Ana **ⓣ** 958 22 59 90 **ⓦ** www.granada.org

Alhambra Tickets can be bought on the day but it is advisable to book in advance by calling **ⓣ** 902 22 44 60, visiting any branch of the BBVA bank, or visiting **ⓦ** www.alhambratickets.com **ⓛ** 08.30–18.00 Jan, Feb, Nov & Dec; 08.30–20.00 Mar–Oct

Capilla Real ⓐ Oficios 12 **ⓛ** 10.30–13.00, 16.00–19.00

Corral del Carbón ⓐ Mariana Pineda **ⓛ** 10.30–13.30, 17.00–20.00 Mon–Fri, 10.00–19.00 Sat. Admission free

Madinat al-Zahra

When Muslim Córdoba was at the height of its wealth and power in the 10th century, caliph Abd al-Rahman III decided to build himself a new administrative city-cum-royal residence at the foot of the Sierra Morena that would put medieval Christian Europe to shame. One chronicler speaks of 10,000 men working daily on the vast building site, yet Madinat al-Zahra was to last only 70 years before being sacked in a civil war.

Madinat is the third biggest archaeological dig in Europe after Pompeii and Crete, but only a tenth of its ruins have so far been uncovered. What you see today is a mixture of original remains and reconstruction using modern materials to imitate the originals.

◆ *A Moorish patio in Córdoba*

The most interesting part is the **Salon de Abd al-Rahman**, the only roofed building (towards the bottom of the site), which has arcades of gracious horseshoe arches and rich decoration on its walls and the capitals of columns.

ⓐ Madinat is just under 10 km (6 miles) west of Córdoba off the main road towards Palma del Río, well signposted from the city centre ❶ 957 32 91 30 ⓦ www.juntadeandalucia.es/cultura/medinatalzahra ❶ 10.00–18.30 Tues–Sat, 10.00–14.00 Sun. Free to EU citizens

Osuna

Osuna stands close enough to the motorway towards Granada for it to make an easy place to break the journey. Although not very significant today, in the 16th century it was bequeathed a cluster of monumental buildings by the dukes who took their title from it. To explore the most interesting part, head upwards from the Plaza Mayor towards the Renaissance church, which overlooks the town. Behind it is the equally conspicuous former university, a rectangular building with corner towers adorned with blue and white tiled spires. Down below there is an archaeological museum (Museo Arqueológico) in one of the town's most ancient buildings, the 12th-century Torre del Agua.

Tourist information ⓐ Plaza Mayor ❶ 954 81 57 32
ⓦ www.ayto-osuna.es
Museo Arqueológico ❶ 10.00–13.30, 15.30–18.30

RETAIL THERAPY

Córdoba

Zoco Municipal This pretty courtyard close to the synagogue is occupied by craftsmen and women who can be seen at work in their studios. There's a shop selling their wares as you come in off the street. ⓐ Calle Judios

Granada

Alcaiceria Granada's 'Arab market' next to the cathedral has become one large gift shop selling the typical Andalucian souvenirs. However, there are a few craft shops of quality such as Artesania Alcaiceria (Nos 1, 3 and 10), which specialises in miniature figures for Christmas cribs.

🔺 *The mountains of the Sierra Nevada soar above the Alhambra at Granada*

TAKING A BREAK

Bars & cafés: Córdoba

Taberna San Miguel £ Better known as 'El Pisto', a well-known old bar on a bullfighting theme where tapas are served along with Montilla-Moriles wines (the local equivalent of sherry).
ⓐ Plaza San Miguel 1 ⓣ 957 47 01 66

Bars & cafés: Osuna

Casa Curro £ A bar with a good selection of tapas. ⓐ Plaza Salitre 5
ⓣ 955 82 07 58

Bars & cafés: Granada

Granada is one of the few places in Spain where bars serve a complimentary tapa with each drink – although you can't, of course, choose what you get. Hopping around the bars that serve the best tapas – some old favourites, some recently opened – is a popular way to start an evening. You can tell which places serve the best tapas of the moment because the crowds make it difficult to get through the door let alone to the bar. Good places to hunt for authentic tapas bars include the streets around Plaza Nueva and the streets around Campo del Principe. Four long-established and highly rated tapas bars are as follows.

Bodega Espadafor £ An old-fashioned bar well known for its tapas.
ⓐ Tinajilla ⓣ 958 20 21 38

Bodegas Castañeda £ Near Plaza Nueva. Gets crowded.
ⓐ Almireceros 1–3 ⓣ 958 21 54 64

Casa Enrique £ Good choice of wines as well as excellent tapas.
ⓐ Acerca del Darro 8 ⓣ 958 25 50 08

Los Diamantes £ Specialises in fish and seafood. @ Navas 26
📞 958 22 70 70. 🕐 Closed Sun

AFTER DARK

Restaurants: Antequera
Los Dolmenes £ Just off the roundabout near Romeral dolmen.
For a starter, try Antequera's typical cold soup, *porra*. @ Cruz El
Romeral 📞 952 84 59 56

Restaurants: Córdoba
Casa Pepe de la Judería ££ Tapas downstairs around the patio;
restaurant upstairs. @ Romero 1 📞 957 20 07 44

Bodegas Campos £££ Wine bodega transformed into a restaurant.
A delightful place in itself, but the food is also excellent.
@ Lineros 32 📞 957 49 75 00

El Churrasco £££ The city's classic restaurant is dispersed around
several patios and other pleasant dining spaces. Specialises in grilled
meats. @ Romero 16 📞 957 29 08 19

Restaurants: Écija
Las Ninfas £ A caféteria-restaurant sharing the building (and some
exhibits) of the town's museum. @ Canovas de Castillo 4, Palacio de
Benameji (Museo Historico Municipal de Écija) 📞 955 90 45 92

Flamenco shows: Córdoba
Tablao El Cardenal This venue puts on a flamenco show six nights
a week. @ Torrijos 10 📞 957 48 31 12 🕐 22.30 Mon–Sat

Clubs: Granada

Granada-10 A cinema in the evening which becomes a discotheque at night, playing disco, hip hop, funk, Latin, salsa – you name it.
ⓐ Carcel Baja 10 ⓣ 958 22 40 01 ⓒ 00.30–06.00 Mon–Fri; 00.30–07.00 Sat & Sun

🔺 *The Moorish palace at Madinat al-Zahra*

ACCOMMODATION

Córdoba

Maestre £ A hotel, *hostal* and set of one or two bedroom self-catering apartments close to the mosque, all extremely good value for central Córdoba. Underground parking available. ⓐ Romero Barros 4–6 ❶ 957 47 24 10 ⓦ www.hotelmaestre.com

Casa de los Naranjos ££ A small hotel with just 20 rooms in the old part of the city. Some of the furnishings were made by local craftsworkers. Internet access available. ⓐ Isabel Losa 8 ❶ 957 47 05 87 ⓦ www.casadelosnaranjos.com

Lola ££–£££ Any hotel that dares to advertise itself as 'the most beautiful hotel in Andalucia' must be worth taking a chance on. Each of the eight rooms is individually furnished with a touch of homeliness. Close to the mosque. ⓐ Romero 3 ❶ 957 20 03 05 ⓦ www.hotelconencantolola.com

Écija

Palacio de los Granados £££ Boutique hotel in a baroque mansion with a small pool in the courtyard. Tapas or a full dinner (on request) served in the evening. ⓐ Emilio Castelar 42 ❶ 955 90 10 50 ⓦ www.palaciogranados.com

Granada

Pension Meridiano £ Cheap and central: between the Plaza Trinidad and Plaza de los Lobos, 5 minutes' walk from the cathedral. ⓐ Angulo 9 ❶ 958 25 05 44 ⓦ www.hostalmeridiano.com

Casa de Federico ££ A small hotel near the cathedral in which the interior design is a striking and harmonious combination of old and new materials. ⓐ Horno de Marina 13 ⓣ 958 20 85 34
ⓦ www.casadefederico.com

Alhambra Palace £££ A glorious mock-Mooorish building on the same hillside as the Alhambra and with great views from its bar-terrace (open to the public). ⓐ Peña Partida 2 ⓣ 958 22 14 68
ⓦ www.h-alhambrapalace.es

Parador de Granada £££ One of the most luxurious hotels in the state-run chain, in a historic building in an incomparable setting beside the Alhambra. It's essential to reserve as far ahead as possible, as it quickly gets booked up. ⓐ Real de la Alhambra
ⓣ 958 22 14 40 ⓦ www.parador.es

Osuna
Palacio Marqués de la Gomera £££ Small hotel in an 18th-century aristocratic mansion with a renowned restaurant, La Casa del Marqués. ⓐ San Pedro 20 ⓣ 954 81 22 23
ⓦ www.hotelpalaciodelmarques.com

ⓞ *Busy shoppers in the Santa Cruz district*

PRACTICAL
information

Directory

GETTING THERE
By air

Seville's Aeropuerto de San Pablo, located 12 km (7.5 miles) east of the city, is served by a number of scheduled international airlines, four of them flying in from UK airports. Flying time from Britain is around 2½ hours. For details of getting from the airport to the city centre, see page 48.

Iberia Spain's national airline. Flights from London Heathrow, most European and many other major airports. It, or its subsidiaries, operate domestic flights within Spain ❶ 902 40 05 00; in UK 0870 609 050 ⓦ www.iberia.com
For Iberia's office in Seville contact ⓐ Avenida de la Buhaira 8 (Cecofar building) ❶ 954 98 82 08 ⓦ www.iberia.es
British Airways (operated by franchisee GB Airways) flies from London Gatwick ❶ 902 11 13 33; in UK 0870 850 98 50 ⓦ www.britishairways.com
Ryanair flies from London Stansted and Liverpool to Seville ❶ 954 44 92 32; in UK 0871 246 0000 ⓦ www.ryanair.com
Air Berlin flies from London Stansted to Seville ❶ 954 26 07 03; in UK 0870 738 88 80 ⓦ www.airberlin.com

Many people are aware that air travel emits CO_2, which contributes to climate change. You may be interested in the possibility of lessening the environmental impact of your flight through the charity Climate Care, which offsets your CO_2 by funding environmental projects around the world
ⓦ www.climatecare.org

By rail

Mainline and local trains are operated by the national company RENFE (Red Nacional de Ferrocarriles Españoles). Full details of these services can be obtained from ☎ 902 24 02 02 or ⓦ www.renfe.es. The journey time from Madrid on board the high speed AVE (Alta Velocidad Española) train is 2½ hours.

To plan a rail trip from the UK to Spain, it's best to go through an international agent such as Rail Europe ⓐ 178 Piccadilly, London W1 (nearest tube Piccadilly Circus or Green Park) ☎ 0870 837 13 71 ⓦ www.raileurope.co.uk

ⓘ It takes about two days non-stop to get to Seville from London by rail.

Driving

From any of the French Channel ports, head south to Biarritz and cross the frontier at the western end of the Pyrenees (between Hendaye and Irún) to reach San Sebastian. Turn inland for Vitoria-Gasteiz and pick up the N-I motorway for Madrid at Burgos.

Madrid's orbital motorways take some navigating. Arriving from the north there is no sign saying Seville. The best policy is to go around Madrid to the east on the M40 following signs first for Zaragoza (but don't turn off for that city), then Valencia, then Córdoba. If you're lucky, you'll find yourself heading due south on the NIV motorway through La Mancha (past Aranjuez) and eventually through the spectacular pass of Despeñaperros into Andalucia. Follow the signs for Córdoba and then keep on the same motorway for Seville.

Alternatively, to save driving through France, take a ferry to Bilbao or Santander (crossing 24–30 hours), and drive south to Burgos, then on to Madrid.

Driving around the centre of Seville may take some getting used to and is best avoided in favour of walking and public transport. Parking can be both difficult and expensive. What's more, some people choose to double park which makes the traffic problem worse.

Spain drives on the right and its highway code is similar to that of other European countries, with internationally recognisable traffic signs. The police can issue on-the-spot fines for traffic offences and being a foreigner does not give you exemption. Seatbelts are obligatory and children under 12 should travel in the back.

Speed limits are 120 km/h (74 mph) motorways, 100 km/h (62 mph) on roads and 50 km/h (31 mph) in built-up areas.

Petrol (*gasolina*) is available as *super, normal* (both leaded), *sin plomo* (unleaded) and *gasoil* (diesel).

Car hire

All the major care hire companies have offices in Seville. Rates are competitive, but you can usually get the best deal by reserving a car from home at the same time as making a flight booking.

Avis ☎ 902 13 55 31 🌐 www.avis.es
Hertz ☎ 902 40 24 05 🌐 www.hertz.es
National/Atesa ☎ 954 51 47 35 🌐 www.atesa.es

SOME WARNINGS ABOUT DRIVING

❶ It is forbidden to drive under the influence of alcohol.

❶ Most national driving licences are valid, but it is advisable to have an international driving licence.

❶ In your car you must carry a red warning triangle, replacement light bulbs and a reflective jacket in the passenger compartment to wear in case of emergency.

ℹ When hiring a car you will be asked to show your passport and an EU or international driving licence.

ENTRY FORMALITIES

Most visitors – including citizens of all EU countries, the USA, Canada, Ireland, Australia and New Zealand – require only a valid passport to enter Spain. Visitors from South Africa must have a visa. There is no restriction on what items you may bring in with you as a tourist, but you'll find almost everything you need locally. In Spain you are obliged by law to carry your passport with you all the time in case the police ask for identification.

TRAVEL INSURANCE

Although EU citizenship gives you basic health cover in Spain it is advisable to take out personal travel insurance as well. This can be obtained from your travel agent, airline company or any insurance company. Make sure it gives adequate cover not only for medical expenses but also for loss or theft of possessions, personal liability and repatriation in an emergency.

If you are going to Spain by car, ask your insurer for a green card and check with them on the cover you will need for damage, loss or theft of the vehicle and for legal costs in the event of an accident.

If you hire a car you will be asked whether you want to pay extra for collision insurance. You may already be covered for this by your normal UK car insurance.

MONEY

The Spanish currency is the euro. It is divided into 100 cents or *céntimos*. There are coins of 1 and 2 euros, and of 1, 2, 5, 10, 20 and 50 cents. The notes are in denominations of 5, 10, 20, 50 and 100 euros.

Banks are generally open only in the morning from 09.00–13.30 Mon–Fri, but there are many cash machines in Seville where you can obtain money with a credit card. Credit cards are accepted for payment almost everywhere except in smaller bars, shops and *pensiones*. Traveller's cheques can be cashed in banks and big hotels. Personal cheques are not accepted anywhere.

HEALTH, SAFETY & CRIME

British citizens – in fact, all EU nationals – are entitled to free treatment from the Spanish social security system on production of a European Health Insurance Card (EHIC). Many travellers prefer to take out private medical insurance before travelling to Spain to give them greater choice of healthcare should the worst happen.

Like any big city, Seville has its share of petty crime. That said, most of it is opportunist and a few simple precautions will make sure you are not an easy target.

❶ Watch out for pickpockets in crowed places like markets and bars, and keep your bag across your chest and in front of you.
❶ Leave valuables in a hotel safe, and never leave anything on display in a parked car.

OPENING HOURS

Shops Usual opening hours are 09.00 or 10.00–13.30 and 17.00–20.30 Mon–Sat. In the summer, some shops open later in the afternoon when the heat starts to die down and stay open correspondingly later.

Department stores and other large shops open continuously 10.00–21.00. Shops are generally closed on Sundays except on special occasions such as the run up to Christmas.

Post offices These are generally open 09.00–14.00 Mon–Fri and 09.00–13.00 Sat.

Banks These are usually open from 09.00–13.30 Mon–Fri.

Offices (government and private business) These are generally open 09.00–14.00 and 16.00–20.00 Mon–Fri. In summer, many offices work a reduced day from 08.00–15.00, then close until the next morning.

Museums Opening hours are generally 09.00–13.00 and 16.00–20.00 Tues–Sat and perhaps Sun morning. They usually close on Mondays, although there are exceptions.

Restaurants Mealtimes in Spain are later than in the rest of Europe. Breakfast in hotels is served 07.30–10.00; lunch is 14.00–16.00; and dinner is generally 21.00–23.00.

Entertainment Larger cinemas have several showings a day from 16.00–23.00. Some theatres offer two daily performances at 18.00 and 22.00. Bars for drinking and musical venues are open 21.00–03.00 and discos 11.30–05.00 or 06.00.

❶ If you are making a special journey to a museum, restaurant, etc., always check precise opening times before you set out.

TOILETS

Seville has few public toilets. The most convenient thing to do, therefore, is go into a bar or café – in which case it is polite to buy a drink. Another option is to use those in a department store like El Corte Inglés. There are several Spanish words for 'toilets', the most common being *servicios*, *aseos* and *lavabos*.

CHILDREN

In Spain children simply fit into ordinary life. There may not be many special facilities for them, but this lack is more than made up for by a general tolerance and willingness to help. For instance, you are unlikely to see a 'child menu', but you are also unlikely to come across a waiter who won't go out of his way to make sure a child gets something suitable to eat.

⬤ *The kids will love a trip to the 'Magic Island' theme park*

Ideas for a family friendly outing include:

- **Isla Mágica** theme park (see page 95)

- **The Wheel of Seville** (see page 80)

- **The April Fair** (see page 12)

- **Aquopolis Seville** water park ⓐ Avenida del Deporte, near the
  Palacio de Congresos, east of the city centre ⓣ 954 40 66 22
  ⓦ www.aquopolis.es/sevilla ⓛ 12.00–20.00 Mon–Fri, 11.00–20.00
  Sat & Sun, July–Aug; 12.00–19.00 Mon–Fri, 11.00–19.00 Sat &
  Sun, June

- **Jerez Horse Show** (see page 111)

- **Zoo Botánico** in Jerez. This is the best zoo in the region.
  ⓣ 956 15 31 64 ⓦ www.zoobotanicojerez.com ⓛ 10.00–18.00
  Tues–Sun; closes 20.00 in summer. Admission charge

- **River boat trip** (see page 58)

- **Horse and carriage ride** (see page 58)

COMMUNICATIONS
Phones
Local, national and international calls can all be made from
cabinas (public phone booths) in the street, which operate
with coins or cards. Instructions are written in several
languages. Some call boxes also take credit cards. *Tarjetas*

telefónicas (phone cards) are on sale at *estancos* (tobacconists) and post offices.

You can also phone from *locutorios*, public telephone centres which are quieter and more convenient than phone boxes. Pay at the counter when you have finished your call.

Calls from a hotel room are more expensive than from phone boxes or *locutorios*.

To make an international call dial 00 + the country code + the phone number, omitting the initial zero. Spain's country code is 34. Seville's provincial area code, 954, must be dialled before all phone numbers, even for local calls.

The country code for the UK is 44, for Ireland 353, for the USA and Canada 1, for Australia 61, for New Zealand 64 and for South Africa 27.
For international information ☎ 11825
For national information ☎ 11818

You can also find phone numbers at ⓦ www.paginasamarillas.es (the Spanish yellow pages) and ⓦ www.paginasblancas.es (the normal phone book listing subscribers).

For any other information on telephoning in Spain see the website of the national phone company, Telefonica: ⓦ www.telefonica.es

Post

Correos (post offices) are open 08.00–21.00 Mon–Fri and 09.00–14.00 Sat. The main post office is at ⓐ Avenida de la Constitución 32 ☎ 902 19 71 97. If you just want stamps don't bother to look for a post office; buy them in an *estanco* (tobacconist's). The cost to send a card or letter up to 20 g is 0.57 cents to a country within the EU and 0.78 cents to the rest of the world. After that, prices vary according to weight. Post boxes are yellow.
❶ To send a telegram ☎ 902 19 71 97

Internet

There are several *cafés cibernéticos* (internet cafés) including:

Amazonas Cyber ⓐ Conde de Barajas 6 ⓦ www.amazonascyber.com

Sevilla Internet Center ⓐ Almirantzago 2–10

ⓦ www.sevilleinternetcenter.com

ADS ⓐ San Luis 108 (near Macarena basilica)

Media

The most popular European and US newspapers, including *The International Herald Tribune*, *The Financial Times* and *The Guardian Europe*, are available from *kioskos de prensa* (newsstands) in the centre of the city as well as at the airport. Many hotels have satellite TV piped to the rooms with programmes in English.

ELECTRICITY

Spain's electricity supply is 220 volt, but you may find an anachronistic 125 volt outlet occasionally in an older building, and for sensitive appliances like computers and mobile phones it is worth double checking the voltage before plugging them in.

ⓘ All plugs in Spain have two round pins, so electrical devices from the UK will only work with an adapter. Visitors form North America will need a transformer.

TRAVELLERS WITH DISABILITIES

Spain doesn't have many facilities for travellers with disabilities, but the situation is slowly changing. More information is available from:

COCEMFE ⓐ Luis Cabrera 63, Madrid ⓣ 917 44 36 00

ⓦ www.cocemfe.es

RADAR (The Royal Association for Disability and Rehabilitation) ☎ 0207 250 3222 🌐 www.radar.org.uk

Holiday Care Service ☎ 0845 124 99 71 🌐 www.holidaycare.org.uk

FURTHER INFORMATION

Before travelling to Spain, general information about the country can be obtained from the Spanish Tourist Office in London ☎ 020 7486 8077 🕐 09.15–13.30 Mon–Fri ✉ info.londres@tourspain.es (visits are strictly by appointment)

Basic questions can be answered by visiting 🌐 www.tourspain.co.uk and www.tourspain.es

The main tourist office in Seville is at 📍 Plaza de San Francisco 19 (next to the city hall) ☎ 954 59 52 88

The official website for Seville is 🌐 www.turismo.sevilla.org

There are also tourist information offices at the airport (☎ 954 44 91 28) and Santa Justa station ☎ 954 53 76 26

The tourist office for Andalucia in Seville province (including Itálica

COMPLAINTS

Spain has strong consumer laws and a strict order in which to make a complaint. First, explain to the establishment in question why you are unhappy with its product or service. This will usually get results, but if it doesn't your next course of action is to fill in a *hoja de reclamaciones* (official complaints form). That will set in motion an official investigation, but if you want to see what other options you have, contact Seville's OMIC (Municipal Consumer Information Office) 📍 Avenida Portugal 2 ☎ 954 23 18 22. If you are still not satisfied, you can apply to the European Consumer Centre. 📍 Principe Vergara 54, 28006 Madrid ☎ 918 22 45 55 🌐 cec.consumo-inc.es

and Carmona) is at ✇ Plaza del Triunfo 1–3 ☎ 954 21 00 05
ⓦ www.turismosevilla.org
For information about other places in Andalucia – including Jerez,
the White Towns, Doñana National Park, Córdoba and Granada –
contact the Junta de Andalucia's office ✇ Avenida de la Constitución
21B ☎ 954 22 14 04 ⓦ www.andalucia.org
Andalucia's tourist helpline is ☎ 901 20 00 20

FURTHER READING

The classic book on southern Spain is *Andalucía* by Michael Jacobs.
The Seville Communion by Arturo Perez Reverte (*La Piel del Tambor* in
Spanish) is a novel that conveys the flavour of the city in which it is
set. Prosper Mérimée's novella *Carmen* (the source for the opera)
and José Zorilla's 1844 play, *Don Juan Tenorio*, are both about the
myth rather than the reality of Seville.

For background on contemporary Spain, John Hooper's *The New
Spaniards* is a thorough and readable account of social and political
change since the death of Franco.

> ### SEVILLE CARD
> The Seville Card gives free admission for one, two or three
> days to all the major monuments and museums in the city
> (sometimes with guided tour), Isla Mágica and the zoo. You
> can use the hop on, hop off official Seville Tour bus, take a
> cruise down the river and, if you pay a little more, have
> unlimited use of the TUSSAM public bus network. Show the
> card and you'll get discounts in many restaurants, shops,
> flamenco shows and clubs. The card can be bought online or
> at any tourist information office ☎ 902 87 79 96
> ⓦ www.sevillacard.es

Useful phrases

Although English is widely spoken in Seville, these words and phrases may come in handy. See also the phrases for specific situations in other parts of the book.

English	Spanish	Approx. pronunciation
BASICS		
Yes	Si	*Si*
No	No	*Noh*
Please	Por favor	*Por fabor*
Thank you	Gracias	*Gratheeas*
Hello	Hola	*Ola*
Goodbye	Adiós	*Adeeos*
Excuse me	Disculpe	*Deeskoolpeh*
Sorry	Perdón	*Pairdohn*
That's okay	De acuerdo	*Dey acwerdo*
To	A	*A*
From	Desde/de	*Desdey/dey*
I don't speak Spanish	No hablo español	*Noh ahblo espanyol*
Do you speak English?	¿Habla usted inglés?	*¿Ahbla oosteth eengless?*
Good morning	Buenos días	*Bwenos dee-ahs*
Good afternoon	Buenas tardes	*Bwenas tarrdess*
Good evening	Buenas noches	*Bwenas notchess*
Goodnight	Buenas noches	*Bwenas notchess*
My name is ...	Me llamo ...	*Meh yiamo ...*
DAYS & TIMES		
Monday	Lunes	*Loones*
Tuesday	Martes	*Martes*
Wednesday	Miércoles	*Meeyercoles*
Thursday	Jueves	*Hooebes*
Friday	Viernes	*Beeyernes*
Saturday	Sábado	*Sabadoe*
Sunday	Domingo	*Domeengo*
Morning	Mañana	*Manyana*
Afternoon	Tarde	*Tardey*
Evening	Noche	*Nochey*
Night	Noche	*Nochey*
Yesterday	Ayer	*Ayer*

English	Spanish	*Approx. pronunciation*
Today	Hoy	*Oy*
Tomorrow	Mañana	*Manyana*
What time is it?	¿Qué hora es?	*¿Kay ora es?*
It is ...	Son las ...	*Son las ...*
09.00	Nueve	*Nwebey*
Midday	Mediodía	*Medeeodeea*
Midnight	Medianoche	*Medeeanoche*

NUMBERS

One	Uno	*Oono*
Two	Dos	*Dos*
Three	Tres	*Tres*
Four	Cuatro	*Cwatro*
Five	Cinco	*Thinco*
Six	Seis	*Seys*
Seven	Siete	*Seeyetey*
Eight	Ocho	*Ocho*
Nine	Nueve	*Nwebey*
Ten	Diez	*Deeyeth*
Eleven	Once	*Onthey*
Twelve	Doce	*Dothey*
Twenty	Veinte	*Beintey*
Fifty	Cincuenta	*Thincwenta*
One hundred	Cien	*Thien*

MONEY

I would like to change these travellers' cheques/this currency	Quisiera cambiar estos cheques de viaje/ dinero	*Keyseeeyera canbeear estos chekes de beeahe/ denero*
Where is the nearest ATM?	¿Dónde está el cajero automático más cercano?	*¿Dondeh estah el cakhehroh der beeyeh ler plew prosh?*
Do you accept credit cards?	¿Aceptan tarjetas de crédito?	*¿Atheptan tarhetas deh credeeto?*

SIGNS & NOTICES

Airport	Aeropuerto	*Aehropwerto*
Rail station/Platform	Estación de trenes/Vía	*Estatheeon de tren/Veea*
Smoking/ Non-smoking	Fumadores/ No fumadores	*Foomadoores/ No foomadoores*
Toilets	Servicios	*Serbeetheeos*
Ladies/Gentlemen	Señoras/Caballeros	*Senyoras/Kaballieros*
Subway	Metro	*Metro*

Emergencies

EMERGENCY NUMBERS

There are separate emergency numbers for police, fire and ambulance, but, if in doubt, use the general emergency number 112 to get you through to the service you need.

General emergencies 112 **Fire brigade** 080

Policía Nacional 091 **Policía Municipal** 092

MEDICAL EMERGENCIES

Pharmacies

Minor health problems can often be cleared up by consulting a *farmacia*, a chemist's shop that is indicated by a green cross sign. Out of hours, there is always one *farmacia de guardia* open. You'll find its address posted in the window of other *farmacias*.

Ambulances & hospitals

To summon an ambulance ☎ 112.

Hospital Universitario Virgen Macarena ⓐ Avenida Dr Fedriani ☎ 955 00 80 00 (English-speaking doctors available)

Hospital Virgen del Rocío ⓐ Avenida Manuel Siurot ☎ 955 01 20 00

Hospital Virgen de Valme ⓐ Avenida Ctra. Sevilla-Cádiz ☎ 955 01 50 00

STOLEN & LOST PROPERTY

If you leave an item on a plane, bus or train, contact the company in question and see if it has been handed in. Report the loss of valuable items to a police station. You will need an official form to make an insurance claim.

POLICE STATIONS

Seville has three police forces. The Policía Municipal is responsible for traffic problems and low-level policing. The Policía Nacional is in charge of more serious crime. The Guardia Civil takes care of highway patrols and customs.

Contact the police for information on ☎ 900 15 00 00 or to make a complaint on ☎ 902 10 21 12 🌐 www.policia.es

Main police station 📍 Avenida Blas Infante 2 ☎ 954 28 93 00

CONSULATES

Australia 📍 Federico Rubio 14 ☎ 954 22 09 71 🌐 www.embaustralia.es

Canada 📍 Málaga: Plaza Malagueta 3 ☎ 952 22 33 46
🌐 www.canada-es.org

UK 📍 Tomares: Urb. Aljamar, block 7 no. 145 ☎ 954 15 50 18
🌐 www.ukinspain.com

US 📍 Plaza Nueva 8 ☎ 954 21 85 71 🌐 www.embusa.es

Ireland 📍 Plaza de Santa Cruz 6 ☎ 954 21 63 61

New Zealand 📍 embassy in Madrid: 3rd floor, Plaza de la Lealtad 2
☎ 915 23 02 26

South Africa 📍 embassy in Madrid: Claudio Coello 91 ☎ 914 36 37 80

EMERGENCY PHRASES

Help! ¡Socorro! *¡Sawkoro!*   **Fire!** ¡Fuego! *¡Fwegoh!*
Stop! ¡Stop! *¡Stop!*

Call an ambulance/the police/the fire service!
¡Llame a una ambulancia/la policía/a los bomberos!
¡Yiame a oona anboolanthea/la poletheea/a lohs bombehrohs!

The publishers would like to thank the following individuals and organisations for supplying copyright photographs for this book:
Nick Inman: all photos except
Pictures Colour Library: pages 103, 122, 135

Copy editor: Sandra Stafford
Proofreader: Lynn Bresler

Send your thoughts to
books@thomascook.com

- Found a great bar, club, shop or must-see sight that we don't feature?

- Like to tip us off about any information that needs updating?

- Want to tell us what you love about this handy little guidebook and more importantly how we can make it even handier?

Then here's your chance to tell all! Send us ideas, discoveries and recommendations today and then look out for your valuable input in the next edition of this title. As an extra 'thank you' from Thomas Cook Publishing, you'll be automatically entered into our exciting monthly prize draw.

Send an email to the above address (stating the book's title) or write to: CitySpots Project Editor, Thomas Cook Publishing, PO Box 227, The Thomas Cook Business Park, Unit 18, Coningsby Road, Peterborough PE3 8SB, UK.